EVOLUTION OF MODERN TEXTILES

J N VOHRA

ORIGINALS

DELHI-110052

Distributed By:
D K Publishers Distributors P Ltd.
1, Ansari Road, Darya Ganj,
New Delhi-110002
Phones: 3278368, 3261465
Fax : 3264368
visit us at: www.dkpd.com
e-mail: dkpd@del3.vsnl.net.in

First Published 2000

ISBN 81-7536-192-1

Published By:
ORIGINALS
(an imprint of Low Price Publications)
A-6, Nimri Commercial Centre,
Near Ashok Vihar Phase-IV,
Delhi-110052
Phone: 7401672, 7452453
visit us at: www.lppindia.com
e-mail: lpp@nde.vsnl.net.in

Printed At:
D K Fine Art Press P Ltd.
Delhi-110052

PRINTED IN INDIA

Acknowledgements

I thank my fraternity and friends whose inspiring feed back was valuable in compiling the articles in this book.

Contents

Preface *vii*

1. Textiles through the Millennia 1
2. From Cottage Industry to Factories 5
3. Developments in Textile Machinery 9
4. Changing Scenario of Textile Mills 15
5. New Generation Textile Mills 19
6. ITMA; Olympics of Textile Machinery 23
7. Technology Upgradation; Panacea for Textile Industry 28
8. Garment Technologies beyond year 2000 33
9. Sustainable Development of Cotton 37
10. Cotton Ginning: A Crucial Factor 41
11. Plant Fibres; an Ecological Necessity 45
12. Fibres; Luxurious and Warm 49
13. Wool Marketing Mechanism 53
14. Wool; a perception 57
15 The Traditional Silk Industry 60
16. Handlooms; the Heritage Industry 65
17. Developments in the Manufactured Fibre Industry 70
18. Cyberspace: Information Galore for Textile Researchers 76
19. Moving out of Traditional Work Systems 78
20. Modern Management Methods in Textile Industry 82

21. Computer Aided Management in Textile Industry 86

22. Revamping Textile Education 90

23. Textile Architecture and Interior Dècor 94

24. Health Hazards of Textiles 98

25. Towards Pollution Free Production 102

26. Towards Cleaner Production Paradigm 106

Glossary of words *110*

Bibliography *124*

Preface

This book presents a kaleidoscopic view of technological and managerial developments that are taking place in the day to day operations of textile industry. Most of the references contained in the book are relevant to Indian textile industry. Attempt has been made to arrange snap shot of growth and change of textiles from ancient times to modern age. A glossary of words used in the text has also been furnished at the end of this book.

The book is a collection of articles written specifically for Express Textiles, a weekly publication of Express Group of Newspapers. I started writing these articles during my period of temporary disability caused due to a road accident. Having spent an active life for about 30 years in various capacities in the textile industry, the pause was sickening.

During the recuperating period I took to computer and information technology to keep myself abreast of latest happenings in the field of textiles and other matters relating to technology, industry and economy. This became a productive divergence. The outcome was a series of articles, mainly based on emerging trends and technologies along with retrospection in the field of textiles.

The source of my information for writing articles has been my old collection of books on textiles, besides textile journals and weeklies. Lately I realised that most of the information contained in my collection of books has become obsolete, except for the basics in textile science and technology. Recourse to Internet was refreshing, rejuvenating and an awakening. This coupled with my thirty years of experiences in the divergent field of textiles grew into a storehouse for information provider. My first few days of connection with the cyber space resulted in an article entitled, "Cyberspace; an information galore for textile researchers," contained in this book.

Textile science and technology has been undergoing revolutionary changes. Newer fibres and their diverse applications have been overwhelming the textile industry. Technologies like open-end, parafil and air-jet spinning adopted improvised yarn structures. Texturing, nonwoven and new techniques of fabric finishing opened up new vistas for textile applications. Production speeds of textile machinery kept skyrocketing and crossed the earlier conceivable limits. Microprocessors and computers are overtaking most of the operations of textile machinery with limited interference from the shop-floor technicians and workmen. Dyeing operations are now being performed with greater accuracy and fewer rejects. Maintenance systems of the machinery are being automated. Ready-made garment industry is assuming greater importance. Environmental pollution concerning textile industry is occupying an emergent role. Simultaneously business systems are being overhauled. Information technology is playing an important role to meet ever-changing consumer preferences with 'just-in-time' manufacturing.

All said and done, textile industry is now fast becoming knowledge oriented. To face the emerging challenges of present millennium there is a dire need to rework our textile education courses. Without relevantly trained and knowledge equipped manpower, I fear, the efforts of scientists and technologists to provide us better life in the textile operations may remain unused and infertile. It is hoped that the contents of this book may provide some thoughts to the people pursuing textile profession.

J.N. Vohra

B.Text, M.Tech (Text), F.I.E., C.Eng (I)

Chapter 1

Textiles through the Millennia

As we move into the new millennium, it is time to retrospect the growth of textiles through ages. The story of evolution of modern textiles dates from prehistoric times. There are but few surviving examples of the earliest textiles since textile decay much more quickly than artefacts made of stone or bone. However, archaeological records depicting clothed human figures on earliest cave art and sculptures and other indirect evidences show that human knew the art of making clothing from spun fibers at least 20,000 years back. Thanks to the process of mummification exercised by early settlers near Nile River, and to various textile museums all over the world, which preserved the ancient textiles diligently, today we boast of having better understanding of development of textile art by mankind.

Excavations carried out at various sites throw some light on the origins and usage of textiles in different civilisations. American Museum of Natural History exhibits a rare textiles, discovered in 1993, found at burial sites west of the Dead Sea, dating from fourth millennium BC (Before Christ Era), about 6000 years ago. The textile, made of linen yarn, woven in the basic tabby weave and with dark-brown patterned bands at both ends and elaborate warp and weft fringes embellishments, reflects a very high level of fabric technology that existed even in early times. But before man could weave a fabric, textile materials and the process of yarn manufacturing must have been discovered.

Textile Materials

It is believed that wool fibres extracted from the sheepskin, was the first textile material available to ancient man. There are evidences which reveal that domestication of the sheep took place in South West Asia at the foothills of the Zargos Mountains as early as 9,000 BC. However, the first archaeological remains of domestic sheep were discovered in 1861 in Swiss lake dwellings belonging to 2,000 years BC.

Archaeologists found fragments of linen, in all stages of manufacture amongst the remains of Swiss lake dwellings, which are said to be about 8000 years old. Shrouds around mummies excavated in Egypt confirm the existence of linen fabric made from flax plant in those times.

Similarly pieces of cotton bolls and cotton cloth, more than 7 000 years old, have been found in prehistoric caves in Mexico. Almost at the same time or earlier cotton was also being grown in the valley of the Indus River in the Indian sub-continent. Archaeologists believe that Muslin of the finest weave found from the excavated sites was produced during the Indus Valley Civilisation. The word "cotton" as we know it today originates from the Arabic word "qutun". With the development of Afrikaans as a spoken language it became "katoen" and eventually "cotton". The discovery of silk in China was accidental and is associated with an interesting legend. According to native record, silk existed from sometime before the middle of the 3rd millennium BC.

Textile Art

Yarns and cloth were dyed and printed from very early times. There is evidence of production of printed textiles in India during the 4th century BC. Specimens of dyed fabrics have also been found in Roman ruins of the 2nd century BC. Textile designers of modern era find these fabrics, produced by early weaving techniques, of striking beauty and sophistication. Many decorative arts were also discovered to embellish fabric and cloths. Los Angeles County Museum of Art preserve a burial sheath dates from 300 BC, and is considered to be a masterpiece. The cloth is made of wool with embroidery of cotton and wool threads.

The Chinese knew the art of weaving silk brocade for more than two thousand years from now. Brocade is a woven fabric having a raised floral or figured design that is introduced during the weaving process, usually by means of a set of mini shuttles. In modern days this is achieved by Jacquard attachment. The design, appearing only on the fabric face, is usually made in a satin or twill weave.

'Brocade' is a Latin word which means 'to figure.' Ancient Chinese brocades portray masterful arrangement of numerous Chinese flowers against a background of scrolling leaves. Textiles found in Egypt also indicate a highly developed weaving craft in the Christian era by the 4th century AD (Anne Domini), with many tapestries made from linen and wool. Persian textiles of very ancient origin include materials ranging from simple fabrics to luxurious carpets and tapestries. Some oriental carpets from India illustrate the exceptionally high artistic achievement of Indian carpet weaving during the late 17th through the 18th century AD.

Some ancient arts are very complicated such as Ikat and Batik. These are very old arts. The origin of these arts is still obscure, however, many believe these arts probably originated in India. The term Ikat comes from a Malay-Indonesian word, which denotes a cloth-making process in which threads are resist-dyed before weaving. Grouped in tiny bundles, threads are wrapped in selected areas to prevent color penetration to make specific patterns. Ikat fabrics have been found in India dating to the seventh and in Egypt dating to the 8th century AD.

Batik is a form of resist dyeing, like Ikat, but it uses wax instead of ties to give a resist on the fabrics. Tie-and-dye effects decorated the silks of China in the Tang dynasty dating from 618-907AD. Some swatches of batik have also been found in Chinese tombs that date from 900 AD. The most prominent examples of these arts come from India, Persia, China, Japan, Indonesia, and Africa. Batik technique reached Europe in 16th century AD.

Clothing

Animal skins and furs were the chief garments of human during the Stone Age. Skins of various animals were utilised. Girdle made of flexible shoot of plants would hold them to the body. There is evidence that other than wool, flax fibre was also amongst the first to be utilised as textile material. The chief textile that has been preserved in graves is made of linen, a fabric made of flax fibres. A mummy recently unwrapped was found to have a covering of three miles long of 3" wide linen bandage. Egyptians even believed that the gods were clothed in linen before they came to earth.

During the 3,000 years of the Egyptian culture costume remained a draped style of dress. Thereafter, the Egyptians dresses were influenced by successive conquerors. During some other civilisations such as Sumerian, Mesopotamian, and Rome, dating between 2700 BC to 2350 BC, both men and women were clothed in a large piece of material, most commonly of wool or linen, draped around the body over a skirt. However at about 1539 BC until 671 BC dresses became more complex than before. Now embroidered and carved ornamental motifs also included the dresses. Many scholars believe that initially human designed garments and ornaments for religious or ritual purposes rather than for utility. However, later the most obvious function of dress was to provide protection from vagaries of weather elements, and as time passed an identity or a status symbol.

As civilisations grew human learnt the art of dressing with made-up textiles. With developments in costume designing the trend was to make luxurious and varied attires with rich colours and ornate. In some civilisation dresses reflected a distinct division of social class, with certain colours, fabrics, and styles reserved for citizens and important personages. For example, only Roman citizens could wear Toga, very famous attire under the Roman Empire. Specific members of society wore certain patterns and colours.

Dresses were dictated not only by the standard of culture of the individual groups and tribes, but varied as much as the climate, the terrain of the inhabitants, and the predators they faced. The names of these garments also varied from country to country. Likewise the materials from which they were made varied according to what was available. In general, linen, cotton, and wool were the norm. Later when silk was discovered the well-to-do people always worn garments made from rich fabrics with a silk base. This created a distinct dress culture and evolved a new social order, which became more prominent during Elizabethan era.

The earliest representations of dress styles in Japan are to be found in 3rd to 5th century AD clay grave figures. A few of these figures show men and women wearing meticulously detailed two-piece costumes consisting of crossed-front jackets that flare out over the hips. Men wore full trousers and women pleated skirts. The ancient origin of two of the most characteristic garments of modern India, the Dhoti worn by men and the Sari worn by women, is depicted in the sculptures dating back to the 2nd century BC. The upper bodies of both men and women were unclothed, though women wore a narrow cloth girdle around the waist. In 10th century AD, women were wearing a tightly fitted short blouse, known as 'Choli' under the Sari. No major change in costume appears to have been made in India until the 12th century, when the Muslims conquered northern and central India. However dress in southern India was little affected by Muslim rule in the north. The Dhoti continued to be worn by most Hindu men and the sari by women. After the British rule, the western way of dressing dominated in urbanised society of India.

Chapter 2

From Cottage Industry to Factories

Nature has been the best educator of mankind. Ancient human first learnt the twisting of grass strands to make ropes, imitating the twisting of creepers around the stems of trees. From that beginning, they learnt to twist, or spin the fibers derived from inside the stalks of flax and fibre coats of sheep and goats. From early times through the Middle Ages spinning was accomplished by the use of a device comprising of distaff and the drop spindle. This device is similar to 'Takli', as we know it today in India. The distaff is a stick on which the mass of fibres is held.

Spinning wheel, first invented in India, was introduced to Europe in the Middle Ages. This spinning wheel was later modified in Europe at the beginning of the 16th century, which came to be known as 'Saxony wheel' and is similar to 'Charkha' of Gandhi era. This development mechanised the spinning process. Later in 1770 James Hargreaves patented a spinning jenny with which twenty-four spindles could be operated. A hand-operated machine for carding cotton was also added.

Weaving and its traditions have a history as ancient as mankind. Human first learnt the art of basket weaving. Art of weaving fabrics probably originated from this technique of basket weaving. The earliest evidence of weaving, closely relate to basket weaving which dates from Neolithic cultures of about 5000 BC. The earliest loom dates from the 5th millennium BC and consisted of a frame to hold a number of parallel alternative threads in two sets, later known as warp. By raising one set of these threads a space was made between them to run a thread cross, later known as weft. The block of wood that used to carry the weft strand through the warp was later called the shuttle. Interestingly, the fundamental operation of the loom remained unchanged till date. But long successions of improvements were introduced through ancient and medieval times that gave birth to present day handlooms in its various forms.

Stitching and Sewing

The art of sewing is at least 20,000 years old. Ancient peoples joined pieces of material using bone and horn needles and animal sinew for thread. However, sewing was mostly confined to side seams and, in later years, to armholes. Around the 14th century iron needles were invented, and by the 15th century there were eyed needles. Basic hand-sewing stitches included the running, hemming, and blind stitches. Interestingly, many earlier stitches are still common and more easily executed ones. Later sewing needles were made of steel, as they still are today.

In 1851 Isaac M. Singer, an immigrant from Germany settled in New York, invented the first sewing machine making it possible to sew on any part of the garment. Soon after, he started mass production of these machines. In 1856 James Gibbs invented the chain stitch machine. This invention changed the earlier tradition of home stitching to shop tailoring in Western Europe. Today there are machines for sewing almost every conceivable article, including clothing, upholstery, canvas, and leather goods. In 1873, Levi Strauss, an immigrant merchant from Germany patented a men's work pants with riveted pocket corners made from denim fabric, now known as Jeans, and started a manufacturing factory for the same in San Francisco.

With the emergence of ready-made garment concept tailoring took to garment industry in most part of the world. Lately garment manufacturing processes underwent radical changes. The first hand-powered sewing machines in the 19th century sewed 20 stitches per minute. At the turn of the century some electrically powered machines sewed 200 stitches. By mid-20th century machine speeds reached 4,500. By 1970 most machines could sew 7,000, and some could sew 8,000 stitches per minute.

Art of Needlework, such as in knitting, crochet or Embroidery are also quite old. However the earliest known examples of stitch work date back to 3000 BC. The term or word 'Embroidery' comes from the Anglo-Saxon word for "edge", but the technique itself was being done long before that. The 17th and 18th centuries are considered golden age for western embroidery. After mid eighteen the invention of embroidery machines devastated the hand embroidery industry, causing major economic crises in many parts of the world.

Industrial Revolution

The art of making yarns and weaving of fabrics grew with the necessity of mankind, and as a part of avocation. In England by mid of

18th century, the inventions of flying shuttle by John Kay and power drive by Edmund Cartwright created an Industrial Revolution that changed the scenario of the textile industry altogether. Now operations of hand weaving were largely taken over by power operated looms. Simultaneously in France an invention was made to mechanise the function of raising warp threads in a group as required by the pattern. This invention was named as 'Jacquard' after its inventor Joseph-Marie Jacquard. Earlier these operations were performed manually by a draw boy on a special drawlooms.

The mechanisation and improvements in the weaving system created yarn shortage, which pressed for creating matching mechanical spinning system. The result was a series of inventions that converted the spinning wheel into a powered, mechanised component of the Industrial Revolution. Sir Richard Arkwright, making use of earlier inventions of James Hargreaves' spinning jenny, produced a better machine, capable of making stronger yarn than Hargreaves' jenny. Later Samuel Crompton in 1779 invented "mule" that vastly increased productivity, making it possible for a single operator to work more than 1,000 spindles that effectively put yarn spinning on a mass production basis. Simultaneously in the United States, in 1793, Eli Whitney invented the cotton gin that raised the demand for American cotton whose production until now was inhibited by the slowness of manual removal of the seeds from the raw fibre.

The Industrial Revolution, at its height between 1760 and 1815, also brought great change to people's lives, especially in the area of work. Until now all items were produced by hand and no need was felt for employing large capital or creating separate workstations. The system of working in the cotton industry was slow and tedious. The workers would buy raw materials from merchants and bring it back to him after producing the given item at their homes. Since items were produced all by hand, workers productivity was very low. The Industrial Revolution changed all that.

Soon after the turn of the 18th century the first Powerloom was developed. Later the replacement of waterpower by steam-power increased the speed of power-driven machinery, which greatly accelerated the growth of the mill system that became firmly established, first in England, later in Europe and the United States. Thus the cottage industry slowly changed to factory system that began to blossom in the 19th century onward. New machines were expensive but one who could owe couple of machines and people to mass-produce items could make huge profits. Now one machine could do a work equivalent to twenty workers. This induced a fear in the minds of people that they will be rendered surplus and unemployed. This led to workers unrest at various places in England. However, the early fears of unemployment due to industrialisation were proved groundless as by the middle of the 19th century the new mills were requiring more and more labour.

The Modern Textile Industry

Successions of improvements brought about in textile machinery in the 19th century increased the volume of production of textiles. In the second half of 20th century emphasis was laid on developing fully automatic or nearly fully automatic systems of machinery. Interestingly, modern looms still retain the basic operational principles of their predecessors but have added a steadily increasing degree of automatic operation. Also now better understanding of the structure and physical and chemical properties of fibres facilitated application of scientific principle in the processing of textiles. In the late 19th century, a new realisation that fibres could be manufactured through chemical activity resulted in the development of man-made fibres. These discoveries led to the manufacturing of new textile materials in the factories.

In the 20th century, with the development of electronics and computers, new physical and engineering concepts were employed in textile research and development. In addition to mechanical improvements in yarn and fabric manufacture, there have been rapid advances in the development of new fibres and fabric processes to improve textile characteristics. Simultaneously, new testing methods to test textile materials have been developed, allowing greater control on quality of finished products.

The modern textile industry now employs technicians, engineers, and artists beside machine tenters. Newer fabric construction methods now employed in weaving and knitting are achieving greater acceptance. Rapid technological advances and development of newer materials opened a wider application base for textiles. At this stage we must salute the creativity and ingenuity of early human who invented the technique of spinning, weaving and dyeing arts that laid the foundation of modern textiles.

Chapter 3

Developments in Textile Machinery

When mechanised spinning processes began to be developed during the nineteenth century and at the beginning of the twentieth century, three basic types of fibres were in use namely wool, cotton, and bast fibres. Consequently three basic spinning systems were initially developed. There were thus wool, cotton, and bast fibre spinning techniques. The wool spinning technique was later divided into worsted and woollen systems.

The steady and rapid growth of supplies of man-made fibres brought about the development of slightly 'modified spinning' technique using the existing equipment of cotton spinning in the developing countries. However, in Europe the conventional worsted system is generally used for spinning man-made fibres. Since then many developments have been made in the textile machinery, which has revolutionised the ways of conversion of fibres into yarn and fabrics and also simplified production processes.

Yarn Spinning

The introduction of new technical equipment into spinning mills did not change the basic requirement of the technical processes in yarn manufacturing. However, presently the tendency of the spinning machine manufacturers is to combine considerable number of technical operations to achieve automation of production lines. The example at hand is the processes of feeding the material from the bales, through opening, blending, and cleaning of materials to the carding machines in regular layers by chute feeding mechanism, followed by formation of card slivers with auto-levelling. All these operations are combined in an automated line. Further the intensification of opening and cleaning operations has been a significant development that assured flow of smaller and cleaner tufts. This, in turn, has facilitated the construction of modern cards with many-fold outputs as compared to conventional cards.

Carding output, which until recently was limited to 4 to 6 kg/hour, has been speeded up to even 100 kg/hour in recently built machines. Technically this was possible due to accelerating the operating speeds of the licker-in and the cylinder. This was made possible due to the application of improved web-doffing devices on the doffer with the aid of a suitable arrangement of rollers. Installation of metallic coverings on the main cylinder and doffer, and very accurate regulation of distance between the working elements largely helped achieving higher speeds. Moreover, installation of casings to cover entire carding machine along with equipping the machines with pneumatic and suction devices to remove the wastes from beneath the working organs were also instrumental in increasing the output per machine.

The effectiveness and output of drawing frames for cotton and for man-made fibres have been greatly increased. The operating speeds of drawing frames have increased to 1000 m/min from 40 m/min and are now built as 1-delivery per machine compared to previous 6-delivery machines. Technical progress in drawing frames was not, of course, confined exclusively to increasing their operating speeds. All high-speed drawing frames are equipped with pneumatic cleaning systems for flies and dust. Drawing frames are also equipped with auto-levelling devices. New types of drawing frames, which prepare slivers for direct spinning and deliver the same to normal or special short cans, came on the scene.

The old technology of using multi-stage-roving frames gave way to single stage simplex frames. Modern day roving frames are characterised with increased rotational speed of spindle, which has considerably increased the output of this machine. Yarn package loads on modern roving frames usually fall within the range of 1.5 to 2.5 kg. Sizes of the packages range from 300 mm to 400 mm in height and 140mm to 175 mm in diameter. This has also contributed towards increased efficiency of ring frames.

Thanks to the precision and accuracy of machine building, contemporary ring spinning frames built by well-known machine makers may attain working speeds of about 25000 rev/min. The features of a modern ring frame include single belt for all spindles or a four-spindle drive, hydraulic control of ring rail lifting, improvements in yarn balloon geometry, and precise controls of variable spinning speeds during the cop building. In industrial practice, however, an attainment of this rated speed of spindle rotation is exceptional, because the strength of the spun product is usually insufficient to withstand the variable tensions that occur.

The features of a modern winder have allowed its speeds to increase more than 1600 meters/min from 250 meters/min of a conventional winder. This was made possible due to precise engineering of the yarn path, effective controls in winding tensions, improving the geometry of cone building, and auto positioning of cones and auto-doffing. Further to these, attachments such as electronic yarn clearing and splicing have tremendously contributed towards ultimate yarn quality. Two-for-one twisting, a revolutionary method of doubling the yarn at high speeds completed the scene of modern developments in yarn manufacturing.

Fabric Forming Processes

The growing intensification of the weaving processes require higher quality of sized warp, the quality of which depends mainly on proper and uniform application of size on the yarn. Shirley's automatic size-box takes care of this problem by assuring steady concentration and viscosity of the size solution. Further the problem of warp stretching during the sizing process have been taken care of in modern machines by dividing the warp flow into several zones, in which different stretches and tensions are applied to the warp. The moisture in sized warps is an important parameter in sizing since the output of weaving process depends on it. Control measuring devices are now used, which regulate the sizing speed according to moisture needed.

Until quite recently, the type of sizing machines commonly used was with a chamber dryer. This system limited the speed of sizing because its evaporative ability is low. Furthermore, chamber drying is uneconomical. Replacement of chamber dryer by the multi-cylinder dryer became possible only after coating the first few cylinders with Teflon that solved the problem of the wet warp sticking to the cylinder surface. This improvement has made possible an increase in sizing speed. Multi-cylinder dryers are more economical than chamber dryers because they consume less steam per pound for the evaporation of water from the warp.

In the contemporary period, all types of looms are in operation, the most modern shuttleless looms, automatic looms, conventional powerlooms built in the previous century and even the age-old handlooms. Automatic looms with modern weft replenishment came on the scene in the forties. This led to an increased general output factor and a very distinct saving on manpower.

Further with the emergence of shuttleless weaving machines, the technology of weaving got revolutionised. Presently these looms could operate more than 1000 RPM. Necessitated by the higher production speeds of these shuttleless machines, recent years have seen important developments related to the intensification of preparatory weaving processes also. These modern weaving machines are designed on the basis of conventional power looms with modernised weft insertion system, which was the result of sustained research and studies in the dynamics of the picking mechanism. However, formation of selvages on the shuttleless looms is quite different from the conventional way. Further suppression of noise and vibrations associated with the higher speeds of this new generation weaving machine is still a topic for the researchers.

Shuttleless looms available in the market are of different types; gripper looms, jet looms, rapier looms, projectile looms, circular looms and that of recently developed multi-shed weaving machines. Latest attempts in designing the weaving looms have been to introduce greater versatility to adopt to more types of yarns, fibres and counts besides weaving both lightweight and heavy weight fabrics. Even though, shuttleless looms are characterised by higher output per machine and per operator, these looms are complicated and consequently very expensive. Their high price affects the weaving costs very greatly. Efforts are being made to lower these costs by simplification of loom construction and by making them with fewer components.

Fabric Finishing

In recent times the efforts have been to prepare grey fabric with pre-treatment in order to render it suitable for consistent, reproducible, fault free coloration and finishing. These aspects have received more attention in order to meet the increasing customer demands for quality and consistency. The main developments in the finishing processes have been towards open-width treatment for scouring and bleaching and continuous preparation and dyeing methods. Jiggers and winches are still in use for the dyeing and bleaching of the woven and knit fabrics respectively. With the emergence of man-made fibres, machines have been built with stainless steel enclosed vessels to withstand high temperature and high pressure for shortened process time, impregnation of dye-solution through jet or spray and microprocessor controlled dyeing cycles. Machine manufacturers have also devoted greater attention towards energy saving devices such as built in heat recovery units and low material to liquor ratio processing.

Recent developments in dyeing have been confined largely to improvements in operating techniques with the objective of saving time, energy and thereby money. Thanks to the development of auxiliaries and other modern aids, the reaction times during desizing, scouring and bleaching have reduced considerably. Reactive dyes are taking an ever-increasing share of the market for wash-fast cottons. They are easier to apply, possess better level-dyeing properties and are now fairly cheap. There have also been developments in fabric mercerising techniques on chain-type and in some cases chain-less type continuous machines. The process has helped in producing lustrous fabrics, bleached and dyed, with easy-care finishing.

The age old engraved roller printing has fundamental limitations, more fabric is now printed by screen techniques. This method of printing has encouraged innovation in designs. Well-designed, mechanised flatbed machines give very precise prints and are especially suitable for wide fabrics and large repeat patterns. Rotary-screen printing machines have been proved to be technically and economically most viable. A textile printer can achieve complete flexibility with rotary-screen machine, choosing either to print on to paper and transfer when fabric orders are obtained, or to print directly on to the fabric.

The trend picking up globally is that print runs are coming down and the average number of colours per design is increasing. This situation pushes the capabilities, and economics of rotary screen printing to the limit. This has led to a more fundamental change in the printing technology that has enabled direct translation of digital design information from a computer-aided design (CAD) system into print, without the use of screens. In this way printing could provide quick response to changing demand because there is no need for the production or changing of patterned screen or rollers. Particularly for short runs this would mean a drastic increase in flexibility.

Future Trends

It was not until quite recently that radical change in the systems of mechanical treatment of fibres, yarn and fabric forming occurred. Scientific research and machine building efforts were concentrated in three main directions of developments; those are automated systems of raw material treatment, increase of operative machine speeds, and the automation of certain segments of processing. Of course the capital expenditure on the modern machines have gone considerably high, but these tend to be off-set by lower index of expenditure on buildings, higher efficiency of human labour, lower production costs and remarkable improvements in quality.

Nonetheless, higher output speeds of the textile machines have posed some inherent problems. Machine down times is becoming very costly. Ways and means are being attempted to reduce the stoppages to minimal. Along with increased output efforts are to create built-in maintenance systems without compromising on the quality of delivered materials. Cotton contamination in developing countries has attracted attention of researchers and machine builders. Improvements in the extent of yarn evenness and its hairiness will also be targeted. Greater flexibility in the spinning of count ranges, with built in adaptability and compatibility for material balancing in a spinning mill will continue to bother the machine builders. Microprocessor controls will be increasingly used for quick change over of process and quality parameters.

Chapter 4

Changing Scenario of Textile Mills

The basic manufacturing technology from fibre to fabric has not changed much in the present century, except for innovations of open-end spinning and non-woven fabrics. Further, there has been a revolutionary emergence of a new technology for man-made fibres and the associated efforts to graft and texture the same akin to natural fibres. However, some supplementary technologies augmented the functions of their peers, such as autolevelling, electronic yarn clearing, and weft insertion systems to name a few. In addition, radical innovations that took place in the finishing processes added aesthetic and functional characteristics to the textiles. Newer processes also increased the possibility of widening the range of end-uses of textile materials.

Technology Management

That much and that far are the efforts of machine builders, textile researchers, and concerned scientist. There are indications, yet not sufficient, to show that with the adaptation of the state-of-the-art manufacturing equipment significant change has occurred in the functional style and mind-set of stakeholders, technocrats and shop-floor onlookers. Till recently, functional scenario of a conventional textile mill, barring that of awakened set ups, made one realised the inadequacy in the labour management contents of a professional degree course in textile technology. In the changing scenario, technology management is becoming more of a technical skill, more related to the core contents of a textile degree course. Technical personnel can no longer attribute low production efficiency of a modern textile mill to the machine tenters alone. Previously, in some cases they pushed these workmen beyond human capacity to cope up, say the extent of end breakage in the ring frame department and stoppages in the loom shed. This boomeranged on the management in various cases.

Happily, the electronic monitoring and functional scans built within the perimeters of modern machines and support equipment now limits the rationale of each aspect of textile operation. Workmen, though indispensable component in the Indian textile mills, are at best only an aid in the overall operations of textile technology and material flow, mistakenly labled and pushed previously as technology operators. It is the basics and technological acumen, rather than merely acquired labour control, which now dictate the functioning of a textile mill. Fortunately, freshly turned out professionals from our textile institutions are not lacking in this aspect, and are more poised to take up the reins with an appropriate shop-floor orientation.

Cutting Edge Technology

The technology of electronic yarn clearing and splicing attached to automatic cone winding machines is central to all improvements, downstream and upstream, brought about in the textile processes. Previously, yarns with all type of faults, short, medium or long term could escape into a yarn package. This situation did not provide any guidelines or impetus to the spinners for improving upon the process parameters. On the other hand, in the absence of any fault scans, they took recourse to 'Parta'; manipulating contents of cotton to minimise 'mixing costs' to the last pie to please their mentors, shelving the basic tenets of spinnability and building yarn quality for academic concerns only. This created a vicious circle.

Spinners attributed bad working in the spinning department and poor yarn quality to the negligence of workmen and lack of supervisory controls. Rationale had no place over ostensible immediate gains. Over a period, this became an established work culture in some of the textile mills. Bad working not only produced undesirable quality of the yarn, but also damaged the machine components along with lowering the morale of the work force. Maintenance of the machines suffered. A planned renovation was the last resort, since the stakeholder wanted to 'milk the cow' until last drop before putting in further investments. Technocrats connived with the decisions of the top management, since this was also a convenient cover for their own misdeeds. May be some of these mills had already seen their days and were now groping in the sunset.

Most of the these textile mills with non-professional work culture have vanished from the scene; some closed down, some taken over by government run corporations, others declared sick and at the verge of closing down. True, technical aspects were not the only cause of their degradation but then the mind-set of managers, at the driving seat, percolates down to all functions of a mill with manufacturing as the core activity.

In this degrading scenario one good thing happened. Equipment like electronic yarn clearer attached to automatic winders forced spinners to improve the yarn quality at the spindle point. This equipment, set to desirable limits, will not let the yarn faults pass onto the package, and large number of yarn faults will lower the efficiency of the automatic winders, thereby increase the costs. Moreover, undesirable yarn quality was no incentive either to go for modern high speed weaving and knitting machines, since every downtime of these machines due to yarn faults cost dearly. Maintaining the quality of the yarn to cater to customers that are more demanding became the driving force for further upgradation.

Modernisation Bandwagon

Meeting increased export demand of a quality yarn forced some of the existing mills to go for Autowinders. Simultaneously, some of the domestic manufacturers installed shuttleless weaving and high-speed fine gauge circular knitting machines and required only fault free cotton yarns. Now yarn spinners, once bitten in the export game in the seventies, never wanted to burn their fingers again. Moreover, emergence of man-made fibre technology brought-in a new breed of fibres with negligible or desired variability in length and fineness and without any accompaniment of foreign matters. Now Mills started segregating work areas of synthetics and blends to air-barred departments to avoid alien fibre admixture in the synthetic blends through air routes. Selected and favourite staff and workmen were given chance to work with synthetic blends.

The aggrandisement of synthetic blends provided an opportunity to mill managers to retrain their staff and workmen in better mill practices. This established a new work culture with cleaner and efficient work arena. Things started to look up in those mills. Some of the better-established technocrats became pioneers in establishing and administering this new culture and later they took pride in the same.

Cotton mixings improved vis-à-vis counts spun. They replaced opening and cleaning lines or some of its beating points with better and more effective versions. Draw-frames equipped with drafting systems for better fibre controls and auto-levellers came on the scene, which took care of long and medium term variations in the yarn. They now brought-in high-production cards and replaced outlived card clothing of the existing ones. Ring Frames found improved versions of drafting systems with needle bearings in the bottom rollers. Now they replaced outdated spindles with latest versions, installed effective pnumafils to cope up, and variable speed motors to contain end breakage. Now everybody wanted to ride on the modernisation bandwagon.

Another significant addition in the spinning mills, that is, two-for-one twisters for preparing a knot-free doubled yarn package now fully paved the way for modernisation in the down stream units. Up-to-date automatic looms replaced conventional power looms. High-speed Sizer equipped with multi-cylinder dryer with Teflon coating replaced conventional Slasher sizing. Warpers were now equipped with magazine creels and electrical stopped motions.

Processing units installed high temperature and pressure-dyeing machines to dye synthetic blended fabrics. Continuous open-width bleaching ranges started replacing batch processes. Mechanical shrinking range formed an essential component in the fabric finishing lines. Engraved roller printing gave way to flat bed printing and rotary-screen printing.

Mills prepared elaborate modernisation schemes and submitted to the financial institutions for term loans. The techno-economic feasibility of the modernisation showed good profits to cover on-going losses and interest liabilities. The exigency to cope up the quality and productivity levels for justifiable returns of the modernisation costs became the dictum of the day. Gradually, the functional scenario of some textile mills of India started changing for the betterment.

Chapter 5

New Generation Textile Mills

Thanks to the liberalisation in the early nineties and hundred per cent export oriented units (EOU) scheme launched by Government of India, mills could now import duty free entire set of state-of-the-art textile equipment. Simultaneously, a new form of integrated and product specific industries, such as terry-towel, denim, knitted fabrics and garments, came on the scene. In addition, they installed open-end spinning machines mainly to consume wastes from the spinning mills profitably. With the opening up of the economy in nineties, first generation entrepreneur, new to the field of textiles, also set up new units. Some of them graduated from small-scale industries, others diversified from different industrial segments, and some were traders and even professionals from various fields.

Initial Euphoria

Finding support from the government in the form of incentives and loans from the financial institutions, most of the entrepreneur opted for 100 per cent export oriented units to catch up the export verve. Some of these plants were set up in joint collaboration with the state industrial corporations, thus adding substantially to the promoter's contribution. This also provided opportunities to the existing enterprises to expand and diversify their product range. Second and third generations of the existing industrial houses also ventured new textile projects.

Ironically, the initial euphoria of establishing industries subsided at the fag end of this very decade in which it erupted. They have attributed various causes to the same including public issue debacles, unnecessary regulatory controls, unpalatable fiscal policies along with frequent change of governments, industrial recession, shrinking economy of EU and the upheaval in the South Asian currencies. Nonetheless, a new era of hi-tech in the Indian textile mills had begun.

Automation is replacing manual operations through the manufacturing sequence of yarn, fabric and wet processes. Furthermore, newer machines with shortened processing cycles are coming. Mills have also improvised material handling equipment. Developments made in the waste management, controls over atmospheric conditions, and general ambience of functional areas of a textile mill are now more conducive to efficient working. This coupled with highly proficient machines engineered for higher production speeds has changed the work culture of a textile mill altogether. This should also be sufficient cause to prompt our R & D institutions to have a fresh look into the outdated quality standards and productivity norms of Indian spinning and weaving mills. The standards and norms should work as benchmark rather than merely a reference to an average of achieved norms by the member mills.

Technology at Work

Duty free imports of textile machines for 100 per cent EOU brought-in large scale of hi-tech equipment to enable make international quality of yarns, fabrics and garments. Ring spindles are working unto 25000 rpm and air-jet looms with 750 PPM. Some of these machines have built-in run-time monitoring systems; remote efficiency displays and reports printing. Mills have incorporated these systems in spinning and weaving departments. Data provided by these computer controlled monitoring included machines with high stops, low efficiency machines, down machines, standing time per machine, operator graph of efficiency, payroll information per operator, and production data.

On demand, these machines can have automatic adjustment of speed controls for pre-determined breakage rate, stoppages and quality parameters due to mixing faults, non-compatible process-parameters or workroom disturbing ambient conditions. If desired, they display this data continuously on large room-wide displays so that operator can monitor his or her own production performance for comparison and motivation. Thanks to the automatic monitoring of quality parameters, now managers can compare the produced quality with the specific quality profile on run-time. Detection and interpretation of periodic faults and probable causes has also become easy. It has also drastically reduced the routine testing of materials and saved testing laboratories from handling extensive amount of data for quality control and management information.

This type of technology at work in the textile mills demands utmost technical skill of the supervisory staff more than the skill of workmen. It also eliminates the chances of the workmen tempering with the mechanical production meters. A workman will not now take punishment or allow his wages to suffer because of technical faults not attributed to him or beyond his capability to mend.

The inclusion of computerised colour matching and recipe prediction system enlivened the rather reclusive and inapt functions of yarn and fabric dyeing departments. Now recipes of shades with alternatives based on cost or performance are available without any time consuming laboratory work. Dyeing procedures; such as start, add, fill, ramp, hold, reverse drain and extract cycles are also built on the lab computer and when needed easily download to the process control computers of dyeing machines. Auto controls now run the processes at optimum speeds and stop precisely when needed to prevent chokes, etc. The setting of all these process parameters are now in the hand of shop-floor managers.

Beyond Technology

The opening up of the Indian economy acted as a boom for foreign textile machine suppliers. This was to the determent of indigenous machinery builders who did not upgrade their manufacturing facilities to match features with imported machinery, or could not meet rapid and short delivery demands of export oriented units. Moreover, installation of world class imported machinery became an assurance for consistent quality deliveries to foreign buyers with whom mills entered buyback arrangements. Duty free cost of the machinery was also a favourable factor for imports. Many world class machinery suppliers entered Indian market.

Simultaneously the cost of textile mills went enormously high over a period. Presently, a cotton mill of 25000 spindles with sophisticated imported machinery from Europe may cost over Rs. 70 crores at prevalent exchange rates. A denim plant with 10 million meters fabric per annum may cost over Rs. 150 crores, and a cotton knitted fabric project with 6 tons daily production may cost over Rs. 35 crores. Having lost the competitive edge to the South East Asian countries in the International market, the economic viability of these high cost projects in India is now more vulnerable to economic volatility.

However, in the meantime, small-scale producers may find solace in what the authors of Beyond Quality, a UNIDO publication, argue. Using case study material from Latin America, Africa and Central Europe, the authors demonstrate that it is the skill and organisation of people, rather than sophisticated equipment, which determines growth in productivity and product quality. They add that these new forms of improvement are not dependent on economies of scale and so provide small producers with the flexibility to compete effectively against mass producers.

Chapter 6

ITMA; "The Olympics of Textile Machinery"

The International Textile Machinery Association show, ITMA '99, the last of the mega events of textile machinery of the millennium ended on 10th June 1999 in Paris. Ever since its investiture in Lille in 1951, the forward-looking entrepreneurs connected with textiles and well-placed textile technologists eagerly await this four-year event. Further this exhibition is very important for the textile machinery industry to show its latest developments, newer models and innovations in the textile production technologies, coincidentally ushering in technological trends over the next four years and beyond.

Even though, in this ITMA the number of visitors to the exhibition may have fallen short of expectations due to global recession, yet the event remained no less an attraction for the concerned persons than the other mega event, World-Cup Cricket played simultaneously in the United Kingdom. Notwithstanding recession, most progressive textile machinery companies exhibited genuine innovation on show, which surprised many.

Indian contingents consisting of corporate heads and technocrats always participated in ITMA shows in ever increasing numbers. Bureaucrats and other government officers at decision making level, even though remotely connected with textile industry, would also avail this opportunity to make a visit to this technology show in foreign countries. Interestingly, technocrats from India have been visiting the exhibition even when hardly any textile machinery was imported, that being in restricted list or attracted prohibitive custom duty in those years. Those visits mostly remained of academic in nature.

After liberalisation of the Indian economy large number of orders for the textile machinery were finalised during ITMA shows. Further, about 40 machinery and accessories manufacturers and suppliers from India put up their stands in ITMA '99 in Paris, the largest participating number from Asia, exceeding even Japan at 32. There are indications that participation by Indian textile machinery industry will grow both in number and essence in the future ITMA shows.

The Driving Force

Lately, the textile market has become more and more demanding asking for better technology, better productivity, and required quality standards, and at the same time lower prices. To meet these unified multifarious demands of the industry it requires great acumen and consistent R & D efforts on the part of machinery manufacturers to incorporate those innovations that are justified both economically and qualitatively. Thus the core of the ITMA exhibition is the innovations carried out in the textile machinery largely by industrially advanced European manufacturers, during a four-year period. Each prestigious manufacturer is in the race to excel others. This becomes the biggest driving force for ITMA shows.

In addition, the show has come to be recognised as a meeting place for business and joint ventures. Everybody who matters in the textile industry would like to be seen at ITMA venue. Now major decisions for the selection and purchase of the machinery for new or existing projects are taken during ITMA. The ITMA '99 event became exclusive since the Exhibitors undertook not to exhibit machinery or models in fairs, exhibitions, shows national or international events other than ITMA until the end of the year. However, these restrictions were not applicable to auxiliary machinery and accessories.

Innovation Galore

It was during ITMA in Milan in 1959 that the technology of texturing of filaments through false twisting was unveiled, and the technology of spinning on rotors was introduced for the first time in ITMA in Basel in 1967. Similarly ITMA 1987 in Paris saw introduction of computerisation in textile industry along with on-line checks in yarn production. In the year 1999 fair, besides some new innovations it was furtherance and consolidation of the concept of automation, on-line monitoring and information systems. Further it was good to observe that some of the manufacturers restricted only to operator friendly and quality assuring features in their machines having already attained higher speeds and productivity levels.

ITMA '99 saw variation in ring spinning system like REITER'S K40 ComforSpin Machine, MURATA'S Vortex spinner, ZINSER'S Air-Com-Tex 700 compact spinner, and the SUESSEN'S new EliTe® Spinning System. The yarns spun from these systems are claimed to be superior to conventional ring spun yarns, having better strength, lesser hairiness, lustrous, softer, pilling resistant with better dye uptake and print definition. SCHLAFHORST exhibited its new Corobox SE 11 with an automatic rotor-spinning machine Autocoro 288 with 48 spinning positions. The machine claimed to spin at rotor speeds up to 150.000 rpm and that too with reduced energy consumption. All these are revolutionary advancements in cotton yarn production.

In weaving, it was now commercial version of the multiphase machine MB 300 displayed by SULZER TEXTIL. Earlier a prototype version of this machine was exhibited in ITMA 1995. The manufacturer claimed that the machine is flexible to adopt to expanded fabric styles and higher output. TSUDAKOMA displayed its new Terry Air Jet Loom. The machine shown is capable of producing the finest jacquard towel at high speed and features the needle-less tuck-in device considered to be the best innovation on the machine. Then there was improved model of GÜNNE Rapier double pile weaving machine with new electronic Stäubli dobby for weaving upholstery plush fabrics. An interesting innovation was exhibited by EVS engineering that could change the face of the fabric inspection methods. The revolutionary equipment was I-tex 2000 automatic inspection system with shade variation analyser claimed to inspect fabrics at 300 m/min working speed. They also exhibited the Loomtex automatic on-loom inspection system, which detects defects as they occur on the loom with full central computerised control through a single computer.

In processing, many exhibitors assured high dependability in textile processing systems and reproduction of exacting quality standards. Human errors are eliminated as far as possible, they claimed. Leading exhibitors were BRÜCKNER with its open-width and continuous dyeing and bleaching ranges and GASTON COUNTY Dyeing Machine Company with its Sentinel™ Controller integrated with SuperTex™ dyehouse information management system. KUSTERS featured its revolutionary fiberkleen technology. The machine optimises the performance and properties of spun yarns and continuos filament yarns during the carpet manufacturing process. The fiberkleen system will provide manufacturers with control of pilling, fuzziness and ability to process both cut and loops carpets. Then there was MONFORT'S 5000 twinair plus-stenter, a new design with energy conserving devices. Most of the features of the processing machinery seem to have accommodated the growing demands for minimum environmental impact besides energy saving devices. Manufacturers claimed global service network, guaranteeing short installation time, careful commissioning and rapid on-site assistance.

Shadows of Global Recession

ITMA '99 happened at a time when the industry was already reeling under the impact of global recession. Textile machinery sales in 1998 were badly affected due to the combined effect of Asian and Russian slumps. Even Switzerland, with its giant textile machines building enterprises, could not prevent suffering a setback in their sales last year. Reportedly, in 1998 textile machinery exports from Switzerland decreased to SFr. 2367 million, a drop of 11% compared to the previous year. The reasons reported to be lesser off-takes in the most lucrative markets in the regions of Southeast Asia, China, and the Indian subcontinent. Further, Turkey which has been an enormous market dropped out altogether in 1998.

Many machine builders viewed the costs of the exhibition of their machinery at ITMA '99 in Paris as an unwanted financial burden rather than a potential investment catalyst. It was reported that many companies though initially registered dropped out from the exhibition. The good news was that undaunted by global recession all major companies registered their presence in that ITMA which showed their commitment to the textile machinery manufacturing. Italy was present with over 300 exhibitors followed by Germany with 260 and Switzerland with 84, UK with 68 and France with 62 exhibitors. Some of the companies made good business deals. Rieter announced during the exhibition that they received an order for over 100 million Swiss Francs, the largest order ever placed at any ITMA, from Hualon Companies.

Menace of Counterfeiting

A controversy, that precedes the holding of ITMA '99, is copying of the machine features by some unscrupulous manufacturers. Counterfeiting of fashionable textile goods has been prevalent since many years. Lately this menace has entered in textile machinery too. Earlier machine manufacturers have been showing only subtle variations in technologies for producing similar end products. But now, as reported some of the products of reputed machine builders such as Jakob Muller, the leading producer of narrow width fabrics, and Santex, leading manufacturer of knitgoods finishing equipment, were copied verbatim. The culprit companies are said to have spent no money on the developments of these machines and do not posses any R & D units of their own. The latest victim being Xorella.

A European Company has openly imitated Contexxor, the unique yarn-conditioning unit of Xorella. Sadly, it was reported that an Indian company also started to sell Contexxor like equipment. Fear of being copied cast its shadow on the Exhibitors in ITMA '99. Due to these incidents many companies were reluctant to give a preview of their latest developments or to exhibit their machinery. They preferred to show videocassettes of their products on the occasion. Some International regulatory agency must check this menace of copying before it takes alarming shape to the discouragement and detriment of those enterprises, which spend fortunes on R & D.

Chapter 7

Technology Upgradation; Panacea for Industry

We have seen in the past that textile companies, which failed to upgrade with the latest technologies, lost competitiveness or withered away. As on August 1999, 285 textile mills closed down in India. The future poses even greater challenges than the past. The ground rules of manufacturing have changed and hitherto great prosperity, which some textile mills of India enjoyed over the last 50 years, may no longer ensure future competitiveness. In the emerging scenario the customers are demanding higher quality, more competitive prices, wider selection of products, and quicker response to changing needs.

Now in order to be successful, manufacturing companies must be able to produce large or small quantities of world-class products, rapidly and economically, in response to market demand, more so in the post WTO scenario. In view of this the textile industry of India has to undergo a dramatic transition from the past systems to a more agile manufacturing paradigm of the future. It is envisaged that such a system should have built-in flexibility to switch from one product to other with minimum time and waste, whether it is spinning fibers, weaving fabrics or apparel manufacturing. Beside, stringent environmental regulations will pose additional stress on the manufacturing systems. Under the circumstances, information sciences and automation, the two vital components of newer technologies hold the key to the future of textile industry of India.

Upgradation Scheme

It is highly appreciable that the Ministry of Textiles, Government of India recognised the need of the textile industry to upgrade. Various factors including the coming into existence of WTO has underscored the need for modernisation and technological upgradation of this sector. Accordingly government established the Technology Upgradation Fund (TUF), which came into effect from 1.4.99 and shall remain effective for five years. According to the scheme, government will provide an interest incentive of 5% points on loans availed from financial institutions during the next five years, and the Ministry of Textiles will monitor and review the implementation of the scheme. This may be a golden opportunity for the textile industry to upgrade with the cheapest finance, at par with the international level, made available during the recent times.

The TUF scheme envisaged that textile industry would utilise to their advantage 5 per cent cheaper capital for modernising or expanding the existing facilities with the state-of-the-art technology or setting up new units with appropriate eligible technology. The scheme covered a vast spectrum of textile industry including SSI. Even though the scheme was launched at a time when the industry had been reeling under the pangs of recession, reportedly the response to the scheme started picking up. Ministry of textiles had done its bit, now it was the turn of financial institutions to play their part by sanctioning the loans to the aspirant entrepreneurs. Reportedly some of the financial institutions were reluctant to have more exposure in the textile industry, particularly Greenfield projects, having already large number of NPAs in this industrial segment. This position of the FIs could retard the technology upgradation process of the textile industry, so spiritedly initiated by the textile ministry. Along with this perhaps an opportunity to restore the diminishing percentage of Indian textiles in the international trade may have been lost.

Excess Capacity Trap

There was an apprehension that with the level of technology expected to be installed under the TUF scheme the industry may build up enhanced capacity unintentionally even with one-to-one replacement of existing machinery, necessitated by economic viability, without any virtual expansion. For example, conventional spindles running at 10,000 rpm are to be replaced with 16,000 RPM and a loom operating at 120 PPM with 400 PPM or more, thereby adding to the existing production capacity. Moreover, many existing as well as new entrepreneurs may put up new units of particular type because others in their knowledge and vicinity happened to be successful in that line. Excess capacity built up in denim and terry towel industries was an illustration. Similarly more than 50% of the wool scouring capacity built up in the country became idle long back. Recently as on August 1999, we have seen the closure of more than 80 lakh spindles, 25 thousand rotors and more than 60 thousand looms.

Demand and supply balances out automatically, more effectively, during recessions. In the absence of any creditable survey on various textile segments, based on domestic demand and exports projections, the repeat mistake of building up or reviving the excess capacity in certain segments could not be ruled out. In that case the competitive edge which technology upgradation provides may be lost. Office of the textile commissioner being in-charge of operation of the scheme should provide safeguard against such an eventuality.

Upgradation of Powerlooms

Powerloom industry is the backbone of textile industry of India since it meets almost 60% of the country's requirement of fabric. Moreover, a conventional powerloom unit has the inherent flexibility to accommodate smaller lot size and shifting from one sort to another with little operational value losses. In one way such a production system could be an asset to meet the ever-changing customers' requirement. The only constraint being that this segment of the textile industry is more prone to quality lapses during production and handling of the materials.

On the other hand the economic viability of shuttleless weaving lies in longer lot sizes and lesser loom stoppages. It is difficult for large number of powerloom units to work on continuous basis all the year around since they work on job basis. Further shuttleless weaving require strong preparatory for its rated performance. In addition some of these looms require purified compressed air for operation, regular maintenance and much cleaner working atmosphere. Above all, there is hardly any base of manufacturing of these machines in the country. Thus entrepreneur will require importing these machines at high cost, which may become an inhibiting factor for a powerloom unit to upgrade.

Under the circumstances the units with old and dilapidated powerlooms might seek replacement with indigenously made looms with automatic weft replenishment; effective warp and weft stop motions and other necessary attachments. To maintain consistent quality it is important that they ensure use of high quality yarns, use higher grade of loom accessories, improvise machine layouts and material handling, have open spaces to stock raw materials and finished goods, install adequate humidification system, and maintain cleaner atmosphere at the work place. Simultaneously they should install modern communicative facilities to keep effective liaison with their customers. These steps are essential components of technology upgradation. In view of this, it may be necessary for some of the units at various powerloom centres to relocate. This may also be truer for hosiery units in Ludhiana and Tripur. TUF scheme should have provided adequate incentives on loans for building new sheds at par with plant and equipment to encourage badly located units to come out in the organised industrial areas.

Sustainable Modernisation

Further one of the main requirements for a unit to qualify for a sanction of assistance under the scheme is competent management. Financial Institutions will like to ensure that competent professionals are available with the unit to carry out modernisation programmes and manage the operations of the unit effectively. Rightly so, since many units, new or upgraded on earlier occasions failed to produce results not because of the deficiency in the installed machinery to deliver, but due to the inadequacy of the management to handle men and material. Such companies, though public limited continues to manifest ownership syndrome.

Some of these units desirous of obtaining modernisation assistance, in one way or the other, manage to meet the stipulation of providing professional outlook to their management. They should realise and appreciate that continuation and retention of qualified professionals is essential for their long-term success. Small-scale units may be taken out of this preview since they are dependent on institutionalised technical support and may not be able to afford professionals.

Earlier we have seen that piecemeal modernisation programmes were not sustainable. Modernisation of most of the textile units belonging to National Textile Corporation and some private units suffered on these accounts. For example the positive effects on productivity and quality with the replacement of key components of ring frame were short lived with unkempt preparatory to feed it and inadequate atmospheric conditions to support it. Induction of only Auto-coners in an otherwise dilapidated yarn-manufacturing unit had little beneficial effect. High production looms with conventional preparatory systems had no apparent advantage in quality and economics of the unit. The lesson learnt was that the technology upgradation has to be viewed in the overall production chain of a textile unit, rather than in the isolated segments, since the flow of textile processes are inter-dependent. Most of the benchmarked machinery eligible under the TUF is required to be imported. Any ill-conceived technology upgradation programme by the units could be unnecessary burden on our precious foreign exchange reserve, without any durable advantage to the industry. And in such cases, technology upgradation instead of being panacea becomes the cause of a chronic disease.

Chapter 8

Garment Technologies Beyond Year 2000

In the last decade, technologies associated with garment production underwent a remarkable change. Computers made perceivable inroads into every aspect of garment manufacturing that is textile design, fashions, embroidery, and production technique and planning. From design development stage through pattern making, grading, lay planning, marking and bulk cutting, partly in stitching, almost in all departments computers perform these functions automatically. It is highly unlikely that a robotic device in the garment industry will ever replace stitching operations, due to its complexities. Thus, in the near future this industry will continue to be labour intensive and remain a domain of developing countries. Nevertheless, one can't deny the incredibility of computer application to the clothing industry. For the buyer it has meant a wider choice of merchandise; for the designer it opened new vistas; for the manufacturers it provided speed, quality and cost saving. The manufacturer was now facing ever-increasing pressure to adopt some degree of computerisation.

The garment exports from India have exhibited an exceptional growth record by any standards. Garments represent the largest net foreign exchange earner for India. Still the superior performance of other developing countries, especially China, provided adequate proof of the large opportunities, which Indian exporters were unable to tap adequately. The ongoing global recession, the South Asian crises and US sanctions, notwithstanding, Indian exporters have fixed an annual export target of rupees 40,000 crores in year 2002 from its present level of rupees 17,000 crores. This was beside the knowledge that the international competition is becoming tough. It will be more so after quota free regime. On the other hand, the global concept of garment production is changing very fast. India can not afford to escape its impact. Serious exporters will have to leapfrog to adopt newer technologies to cope up the challenges of 21st century world scenario.

Mass Customisation

Customer expectations for very timely delivery led the RMG industry to flourish. However, in the process, custom fit sizes were a casualty. Marks & Spencer, the large operator in retail market offer wider size range based on height and girth that is short, medium, tall and very tall within a size chart of small, medium and large. However, there is a limit to the sizes offered. The fact is that everyone has their own size, just like a finger print, and by definition it is impossible to mass produce garments to fit everyone. In developed countries, companies dealing in RMG have realised that in order to stay in business they have to meet both requirements that is ready delivery and custom fit sizes. Moreover, an unstable economic climate, changing consumer needs, and the technologies that are evolving on the scene have created turbulence in the marketplace. Companies can no longer continue to do business without considering the impact of the turbulence.

Obviously, the driving force in this new marketplace is the consumer. The driving factor is technology. This has evolved a new production system named as Mass customisation. This simply means "the ability to customise products while manufacturing at mass production speeds without compromising a company's competitive cost structure." Mass customisation is a broadly based term encompassing vast changes in manufacturing, distribution, and delivery of products. Various researchers at Auburn University, USA are involved to build such a model

One thing is sure that mass-produced clothing will always be cheaper than clothing produced on an individual basis. Researchers are of the view that digital information combined with evolving technology in process manufacturing will allow customised apparel to emerge in mass production environment. Amongst other tools, digital body scanners devised by Textile/Clothing Technology Corporation, USA holds promise for such a model to be a commercial reality. These 3-D scanners calculate measurements by projecting light on the body inside a booth. The scan system is a combination of body scanner and video display that will enable you to try your garments even before the clothing is actually manufactured.

According to a survey conducted by wired magazine, these scanners may become common in clothing stores in next ten years. Adidas is already using a digital foot scanner to measure shoe size. They digitally transmit measurement data directly to the manufacturer. In this way the order system at manufacturer end receives and enters individual measurements. They download these images to a pattern making or alteration software program, such as Gerber's AccuMark 'Made To Measure' system, to create a custom-sized pattern. Invesmark-nt of Investronica is another such system. The system flags the components of the pattern that are not available in the file for CAD alteration. Otherwise, the system pulls the pieces required from a database for the automatic production of a single-size marker.

Many manufacturers in USA and France, specialising in men and women suits are using these systems. They also manufactures US Army and Air Force 'made to measure' military uniforms. Beside, it is claimed that these technologies can be put to use, for example in the production of customised uniforms for Police, industrial undertakings, dresses for school children, hospital and other services staff to name a few. All of this could transform the mass production scene. Instead of producing several of the same style in predetermined sizes, all garments will be 'one-off', made to the customer's requirement. The technology of knitting "Whole-Garment" offered by Shima Seiki, Japan is one such example. One-piece total garment knitwear, long a dream of the knitting industry, is now a reality. With its true on-demand knitting capability, this technology offers one-of-a-kind custom-made sweaters.

Offshore Manufacturing

A new trend imminent in global marketing is a remote control over resourcing fabrics, materials and even in garment production. It is almost as if the clients literally run the factories from far away. For example, some apparel companies in United States are using satellite systems to control each aspect of their contractual production in Eastern Europe. Software manufacturing companies are now offering a system that is a real-time shop floor controller. As claimed by the companies, the system manages multiple international production paths for the same product, tracks the actual cost for each path and maintains a blended standard cost of garments. Users of the system have access to the entire database over the Internet. Another software package allows customers to place orders on-line, look into the status of an order, and even review product catalogues via the World Wide Web. Some companies are offering an offshore distributed database system that automatically tracks production data through queues.

Stitching Automation

Traditional technological principles that evolved during the nineteenth century still form the basis of the clothing industry. This technology consists in the mechanisation of hand sewing into a series of separate technical operation. The primary obstacle in this system is that the manual labour continues to play a dominant role. The introduction of special purpose stitching machines has facilitated, in a certain degree, reduction in the number of operations. These machines are double needle overlockers, safety stitchers, double-chain stitchers, zigzag machines, and hemming machines. There are also semi-automatic machines such as patch pocket setter and sewer to jeans, sewing of darts and pleats, elastic attaches to lingerie, plait setter and sewer, and button holing and stitching machines. Some of these machines are computer controlled. Another development in this field is the electronically programmable lockstitcher. This multipurpose machine follows a pre-designed sewing path.

Still there are large manual actions in a garment assembly line. These are transporting, handling and sewing. Time and motion studies conducted by research institutes show that actual sewing time in the assembly of a garment takes only 20 per cent of the total. The rest is made up of a host of other connecting activities such as; transporting the bundles, handling and positioning the piece for sewing, re-threading and machine maintenance. The rather complex construction of clothing products does not permit the construction of machines that attempt to simulate human actions until an alternate production method is available. Researchers have attempted to produce garments by adhesive bonding through ultrasonic heating. These technologies are still in the experimental stage.

In the meantime the attention of the technologists have been to minimise the time of bundle transporting and piece handling in the garment assembly line. Now many CAD/CAM system manufacturers are offering automated conveyor systems that are computer controlled. These systems move the garment parts along overhead rails and deliver the operator at the correct height almost to the needle where it is removed from an easy release clip, sewn and replaced, and moved on to the next operator. Line supervisor can monitor and control in a 'real-time' overview. Investronica, the Spanish company and Gerber technologies of USA, besides others, offer these modular systems. This improves the productivity and efficiency of the garment production in a quick delivery environment. Besides all, Textile/Garment Technology Corporation, USA has developed a knitwear assembly system. This system automatically picks two panels of cut material off a stack, and then matches, aligns, and sews them into a pair of sweatpants. This achievement may pave the way for further developments towards automation of stitching section in this millennium.

Chapter 9
Sustainable Development of Cotton

Since the dawn of civilisation human beings have been wearing cotton clothes. But it is difficult to know exactly how long cotton has been in existence. However, one thing is sure that cotton continues to enjoy dominant position amongst textile fibres from ancient to modern times. In the present times India has emerged third largest producer of cotton, next only to China and USA. Since India is a tropical country therefore cotton, a cool fibre by attributes, will continue to be the mainstay raw material for its textile industry. Presently, India consumes approximately 2.7 million tons of cotton every year i.e. 15 per cent of the total cotton consumed in the world. USA and other main producers of cotton have developed modern technologies for cotton cultivation and fibre production, regrettably, India continues to depend on old technologies.

Lately global cotton textile industry is facing a tough competition from man-made fibres, having lost ground both on prices and product variety. Global cotton industry, in its pursuit to retain prime position, is making all out efforts to face the challenges of manufactured fibres. Newer technologies are being developed to produce and process cotton profitably. Various finishes have been researched to enhance the maintainability of cotton textiles, and innovative products have been developed to meet the changed consumer preferences. Indian cotton industry should not lag behind in these areas if it has to earn competitive advantage in the global market. In this regard setting up of Cotton Technology Mission set up by the Government of India was a right step, but the mission delayed to take off.

Cotton Agronomy

The main problems that India faces are low yields per hectare, excessive spray of pesticides, and adherence to conventional irrigation systems. These problems have been highlighted by various agencies time and again. Various solutions were also been offered by the concerned agencies for improving the cotton status. Cotton Corporation of

India recommends the use of certified high yielding seeds and modern drip irrigation techniques on similar lines as farmer use in Israel. The corporation has also undertaken various projects on integrated pest management.

It has been said that the drip irrigation technique reduces dependence on monsoons and allows covering hitherto non-conventional areas also for the cultivation of cotton. Government provides subsidy to farmers to meet the cost of laying infrastructure to adopt this technology. It is high time that growers of cotton in India take full advantage of these schemes. It is expected that modern water management technique will enhance the cotton average yield in India from its present level of 310 kg per hectare to global average of 572 kg, at least in irrigated areas such as Punjab and Haryana.

Secondly, every year large quantities of cotton crop in India suffer loss due to pest attack, plant virus and inundation. Suicides committed by farmers in Andhra Pradesh and Punjab are horrid consequences of crop failures. To avoid pest attacks large doses of pesticides, which are toxic substances, are sprayed in the fields. To complicate matters further, insects are quickly becoming resistant to recommended rates of pesticide application and ever-increasing amounts are needed to be effective, more so with spurious chemicals supplied by unscrupulous traders.

In this emerging eco-friendly conscious world consumer may renounce cotton being most toxic and so unfriendly. Already major textile multinationals such as GAP, Levi-Strauss, Nike and Patagonia are patronising natural cotton for use in shoes to shirts and Jeans. India should seriously take steps to meet the emerging challenges of the world if cotton textiles have to maintain its superiority in exports. All farmers want to produce the highest yield and best quality toxic-free cotton while taking care of the land. How they get there is a matter of methodology and philosophy.

Diagnostic Technology

To face the challenges of eco-conscious world, reportedly some farmers in cotton growing countries are switching to organic cultivation. This sort of cultivation means elimination of toxic chemicals in every step of the growing process, by emphasising natural, biological methods, which have far less impact on the environment. USA is adopting the use of bio-fertilisers, compost, oil cakes and liquid fertilisers. Australia has developed a biological insecticide produced by genetically engineered plants to hold in check large-scale destruction of cotton crops by the attack of boll caterpillars.

Alternatively, USA uses an advanced diagnostic technology employing extremely accurate test kit known as 'Heliothine Test Kit' for testing the percentage presence of bollworm in the cotton crop. The kit has been co-developed by Cotton Incorporated, CSIRO (Australia) and Abbott Laboratories, Inc. This test can potentially save the cotton industry a fortune by avoiding incorrect sprays and crop damage by providing an instant assessment of the infestation at the egg and small larval stage.

In addition, Cotton Incorporated and the University of Arkansas has developed an advanced computer aided crop monitoring system. This expert system for cotton crop management is known as COTMAN. The system uses crop mapping at different stages of plant growth to document and compare plant development and fruit retention to a target value. This allows growers to visually examine crop responses to soil and crop management practices and environmental situations. Besides other things the system schedules insecticide application termination and defoliation according to maturity of the last effective boll population.

Indian agricultural scientists should also adopt/develop such information technologies for crop management to sustain cotton growth. Particularly, the yields and quality of long staple cottons need to be improved by modern crop management systems to reduce cost of production. In future the demand for finer and stronger cottons is likely to increase in India to cope up higher speeds in spinning, weaving and knitting. Simultaneously it will also help meeting the increased demand for yarns with lower twist factors for the manufacturing of high quality and soft knitted and woven fabrics for exports. Addressing the needs of customers is very important for the long-range success of cotton.

Product Development

We need to insure that consumers keep demanding better cotton products. Also the positive image of cotton need to be protected through promotional efforts to stimulate consumer demand. Further there is a dire need to grow natural fibres for sustainable industrial development. Cotton is major and important component of natural fibres. Attention of the researchers and development bodies is required not only towards eco-friendly plant cultivation, productivity improvements but also in product development. Cotton promotional agencies should chart a programme to continuously supply mills and manufacturers with design ideas for new products. For example in USA, a 100 percent cotton linen-look apparel fabric has been developed that enhanced the appearance and touch of garments.

A wide range of home furnishing fabrics of 100 percent cotton and cotton-rich fabrics and wrinkle-resistant products are the latest results of the textile research else where. Even cotton sweaters are becoming very popular in Europe and USA. Moreover the inherent properties of cotton make it ideal for use in a wide range of nonwoven applications such as home fashion products, table linens, napkins, place mats, pleated window shades or blinds, lamp shades and floor coverings. Currently in USA cotton nonwoven for apparel end uses and disposable products for personal care such as feminine hygiene products, disposable diapers and baby wipes are being tested.

Long term prospective

Cotton, as other textile materials, passed through a crisis of demand due to slow down of global economy in the year 1998-99. China reduced its spindle capacity with the aim of increasing efficiency and bringing the supply and demand for cotton into better balance. Active spindles fell sharply in Thailand due to rise in labour costs during the past two years. Japan pulled out of its spinning capacity, which shrank by nearly 51% during the last six years, simultaneously the imports of cotton also declined by 40% during the same period. Cotton lost considerable ground in India also, the market share commanded by man-made fibres increased from 48 percent to 55 percent, partly on grounds of price and partly with a shift to blended yarns.

Moreover, more than 285 cotton mills closed down during last two years without any replacing units coming up. Most of the remaining units worked below capacity including some exports oriented units. Knitted fabric, denim and towelling units, in terms of volume are important consumers of raw cotton, worked below 40% capacity. Obviously this deteriorating health of the textile sector has affected significantly on cotton consumption. More than this the key problem that Indian cotton continue to face is decline in the profitability both for the growers and mill producers. Taking these problems as cyclic and of short term, textile industry of India should look-forward and prepare itself with a long term prospective to meet the fast changing global scenario and consumer preferences.

Chapter 10

Cotton Ginning: A Crucial Factor

In a consumer driven textile market, cotton ginning in India has become a crucial factor in the entire textile production chain. Quality and price of the end products depend largely on what quality of cotton has been supplied to the spinning units, since raw materials constitutes 60 percent of the yarn cost. Most of the ginning units in India are old; technology obsolete and machinery dilapidated. Until now this area of cotton industry remained highly neglected and devoid of professionalism. One of the reasons is that ginning industry is seasonal. The recent volatility in cotton production and demand added further to its woes. High rates of trash and contamination in Indian cottons are now legendary. One may be dismayed to learn that Indian cottons though handpicked, yet are contaminated, even after cleaning process, compared to the most contaminated cottons of America.

On the other hand textile industry is now modernising and would need high quality raw materials. Ginning units in India should urgently modernise otherwise the very purpose of modernisation of textile industry will be defeated. In addition, there is dire need to improve the cotton handling and processing practices in the ginning units. It has been observed that the ginning units in India normally carry on same ginning process and drying sequence without regard to differences in moisture content, color, or foreign matter. This sometimes results in either 'over' or 'under' treatments. In case of 'over' treatment there is a possibility of excessive fibre damage and higher lint loss and 'under' treatment results in higher residual trash. To reduce the damage and loss of good fibers, gins can base their lint cleaning on the amount of trash in the seed cotton. But sometimes it is difficult for gins to determine how much trash is present in the lint. Besides there is a need to ensure better returns to the Ginners. This can be achieved if they provide value-added services to the Spinners.

Modern Ginning Technology

A revolutionary innovation in ginning technology has been carried out by U.S. Cotton Ginning Research Unit, Mississippi. The system uses computers, sensors and video technology to gin according to cotton quality. Once the color of the cotton, foreign matter, and moisture content are known, the software decides the best sequence of machine, cleaning intensity and drying to get the best market quality and value.

The system automatically measure the quality of cotton at various stages of ginning and kick lint cleaners and dryers on and off and actuate bypass valves as cotton goes through the gin. For example the system determines when cotton needs two lint cleaners and when it needs only one. The system also regulates the performance of gin machinery to effectively control foreign matter removal, fiber loss, and fiber degradation. As the cotton enters the bale press, an on-line system takes the final reading of fiber moisture, trash level, and color, which are then assigned, to the bale. An off-line system measures the micron value of the cotton packed in the bale. Before this invention, assessing the effect that each ginning process would have on cotton properties was nearly impossible.

The system allows Ginners to customise their process for each farmer so as to increase their profits. This control system technology for cotton ginning has been licensed exclusively to Zellweger Uster, an equipment manufacturer under the trade name IntelliGin. Cotton ginning will become more of a challenge in the future. Sooner or later some big industrial groups in India, in their own interest, should patronise/support the efforts of ginning units to modernise. Already a trend has started in USA toward cotton producers and mills participating in gin ownership, whether by co-operatives or producer owned corporations.

Contamination Bug

The other serious problem in Indian cottons is high rate of contamination, both chemical and physical. Chemical contamination is presence in the form of toxic pesticides and physical contamination include fabrics made of woven plastic, plastic films, jute hessian, strings, organic matters such as leaves, feathers and papers, inorganic matters such as sand, rust, metal and wires and oily substances. Keeping cotton free of contamination during harvesting, ginning and other processing is crucial.

It is a matter of great concern that lint contamination has been on the rise during the past few years, at times when the industry is looking for reduction in production and processing costs. On top of this, the problem of contamination by foreign fibres is becoming acute with increasing automation in textile mills. To keep cotton contamination free, it would need some pro-active plan both by growers and ginners. Some spinning units even employ one worker one cotton bale to hand pick contaminants, but this process is subjective and costly.

To great extent cotton contamination problem can be tackled by installing modern equipment in the production lines. This equipment detects & removes contamination from the loose cotton tufts. This optical vision equipment, manufactured by various textile machine manufacturers, is available for installing in the blowroom lines. However, the results of various mills show that it may not be possible to eliminate contamination absolutely at the early stage of spinning process. For example presence of coloured fibres which recently created havoc in yarns exports escape detection by this equipment and even by hand picking technique. Foreign buyers of yarns filed large amount of claims due to presence of 'coloured fibres' in the yarns exported. It was noted that the coloured spots were visible only after the yarns have been knitted and bleached.

To meet such an eventuality various manufacturers have come up with contaminant sensing and removing devices at various stages of cotton processing, supplementary to the blowroom installations. These devices can be fitted at draw frames and Autoconers. These devices are meant to remove any contamination left behind in the cotton or added during the process of spinning in addition to removing the objectionable yarn faults. But these methods of removing contamination results in productivity losses thus add to the cost. Also it is indeed foolhardy to arrange for removal of contamination, which firstly could have been avoided with little care and handling management at ginning and fibre opening stages.

Cotton Marketing

Cotton is grown seasonally but consumed throughout the year. Annually around Rs. 13000 crore worth of cotton yield is traded in India. One may discover that more than Rs 2600 crores, that is 20 percent of the cotton yield, is still sold outside the regulated markets through middlemen, mostly in villages. Ready cash at their door to repay loans taken from the middlemen lures farmers to adopt this route. Obviously in such cases the farmers are the exploited lots. Concerned marketing agencies should take effective steps against such exploitations and encourage farmers to sell their produce in the regulated markets.

Public auctions based on cotton classification conducted by authorised auctioneers seem to be the best marketing system. This will assure fair price to the farmers for their produce. Woolgrowers in Australia prefer this system. Out of approx. 580 million kilos of clean wool worth $US 2.2 billion produced in Australia, 85 per cent is sold through public auction. Surly part of the approx. US$ 3.0 billion worth cotton traded in India can be managed through auction system.

Other than public auction, recently introduced futures in India seem to be beneficial to both growers and the consumers. Apart for providing an insurance, futures can make planning and budgeting more certain. Unfortunately, in the absence of awareness, this system continues to be a suspect in the eyes of both beneficiaries, consequently it has yet to take off.

Customers of the spinning industry who have made big investments in new mill equipment try to buy better quality cotton. However, conventional buyers still base their purchases on rule-to-thumb methods of tests, which sometimes lead them to wrong conclusions. Mills will like to know all the important properties when selecting cotton bales to use in a mix for spinning yarn efficiently. For example in order to prepare a successful mix and to optimise fibre-to-yarn relationship mill must know CV% of important properties of cotton like length and micron, not only with in the bales but also between the bales.

Indian research institutions should examine the possibility of adopting a computerised system known as Engineered Fibre System (EFS), developed by Cotton Incorporated, USA. The system is said to help cotton buyers analyse critical cotton properties during purchase and Mills can now plan selection of cotton for mix lay downs in blowrooms on the basis of HVI fiber properties. For the selection of bales in a mix a permanent bale identifier have been developed based on gin code and gin bale number, which is maintained through out the movement of bales in the industry. Even specific bale mixes can be shipped directly to the mill based on quality specifications. Reportedly the system has been found to assist mills lower cotton costs, improve productivity and reduce wastes. These value-added services are essential to pop up cotton demand; otherwise mills would look to other fibers.

Chapter 11

Plant Fibres; an Ecological Necessity

Population of the world is increasing and so will the demand for textiles. Experts feel that the demand for textiles will rise exponentially since the disposable incomes are also increasing. In addition there has been increase in fibre consumption for technical textiles, geotextiles and paper. At the same time there has been depletion in the forest resources causing imbalances in the ecosystem. Consequently the pollution problems are mounting, more so, with the production and disposal of synthetic fibres. Hence it is most likely that demand for natural fibres will rise both on account of fashion requirements and ecological necessity. Plant fibres are already gaining attention as an attractive and plentiful source of natural and eco-friendly fibres. Countries such as Japan and Indonesia are already seeking supplies of 'Ecofibres'.

Ecofibres

Ecofibres are bast fibres that extend along the bark of the stems of plants e.g. Jute, Flax, Ramie, Hemp, Kenaf, Sunn, and Urena. Other than these, there are fibres, which come from the leaves and seeds of plants, such as Abaca, Henequen, Raffia, Figue, Sisal, Kapok, Coir and Banana fibres. Interestingly even Banana fibre has its origin in the ancient times. The fiber is golden beige in color, and is harder than hemp. It makes an ideal cloth for tropical summers. There is a mention in the Japanese textile history that both silk and cotton were reserved for the nobility; ramie and banana fibers were the fabrics of the common people.

Recently the group that makes banana fiber has been designated as a "Living National Treasure" by the Japanese government. Presently the global consumption of bast fibres is limited to approx. 1.6 per cent of all textile fibres. There are indications that ecofibres are expanding into current fibre markets around the world. Ecofibres are renewable, sustainable, biodegradable, and can be readily grown in rotation with traditional broad-acre crops, with few inputs, in a broad range of climatic conditions, employing thousands of growers. These fibres can be used for producing all grades of paper, composite materials, and structural building materials, geotextiles beside apparel textiles.

Jute in peril

India is the largest producer of Jute with an average production of 85 Lakh bales per annum. Production of Jute in India exceeds the domestic demand placed at approx. 1200 tons per annum. India exports worth Rs 4700 million of Jute goods per annum. The Jute growing industry is localised in the eastern part of India, mainly Calcutta and employs approx. 2.30 lakhs workmen. In foreign countries Jute is now abundantly used for non-textile uses such as geo-textile in road construction, riverbank protection, shallow land recovery, railway slope protection beside traditional packaging materials.

The use of Jute as packaging material got into trouble in 1990 when Swiss food laboratory reported traces of hydrocarbon in cocoa and coffee beans said to be contaminated by jute bags. The presence of hydrocarbon was traced to the use of petroleum based Batch Oil in the spinning of jute fibre. The Indian industry could overcome this problem with the help of IJIRA (the Indian Jute Industries Research Association). Through intensive research, IJIRA developed suitable non-toxic alternative Batch Oil, based on Rice Bran. Food grade items like Cocoa, Coffee Beans and Shelled Nuts retain their freshness, natural aroma and taste in hydrocarbon free jute bags.

Now Jute is facing tough competition from synthetics especially polypropylene for packaging materials. Moreover hessian cloth used for wrapping cotton bales is found to be one of the cause for cotton contamination. This factor may lead to banning of jute wraps for cotton bales in favour of cotton cloth, which can jeopardise jute market in India. Jute strings for tying bales have already been replaced with cotton strings. Efforts should be made by jute researchers to develop cost effective coated/treated jute wraps to eliminate 'pulled' jute fibres and cut pieces going along with cotton during ginning and opening processes. Recently Jute fibre got successful entrance into blended carpets and apparel uses. The fibre has been blended with cotton and man-made fibres to produce high-grade suiting and denim by Grasim Industries. Efforts should be to produce finer varieties of Jute for apparel purposes.

Flax and Ramie

Flax is perhaps one of the first domesticated crops of bast fibres whose origin can be traced to High-Asian origin, believed to be cultivated first in Egypt and in the Nile Delta. Mummies wrapped in flax cloth shrouds have been found in Egyptian tombs dating even more than 5.000 BC. Flax is a plant, and linen is the fabric made with yarns spun from flax fibers. Linen is fully biodegradable and can be totally recycled. Flax fibre has excellent anti-allergic as well as UV- protection properties. Every part of the plant is used. The crop is best grown in cool wet environments and is best adapted to fertile, fine textured, clay soils. Major flax producing countries are Australia, Austria, Belgium, Czechoslovakia, France, Germany, Ireland, Scotland, and the former USSR. The highest quality flax comes from Belgium, Northern France and the Netherlands. Russian flax is generally weaker but are remarkable for their fineness of fibre. Recently successful efforts have been made to grow Flax fibre in Himachal Pradesh.

Ramie also called China-grass is a woody fiber crop similar to flax. It is currently grown in Southeast Asia, China, Japan, and Southern Europe. Ramie fibres are long and very fine. They are white and lustrous and almost silkily in appearance. The fibre is stiff, more brittle than linen, and highly lustrous. Cloth made of ramie, often mixed with other fibers such as wool, silk or cotton, is used for tapestries, upholstery, trimmings, and towelling. The best-known Japanese 'Jofu' and ramie crepes are the finest grade of ramie fabrics that make summer wear of the highest quality. The technology of making fine ramie fabrics was in its finishing. The fabrics were coated with a vegetable paste and then beaten with wooden mallets for four or five hours. That process gave the cloth a soft handle and silky lustre.

Re-emergence of Hemp

Hemp is perhaps the oldest cultivated fibre plant in existence. It was once the most widely cultivated crop in the world. Hemp makes extremely strong fabric. History reveals that sails and ropes of Christopher Columbus' ship were made from hemp. The word 'Canvas' fabric comes from Cannabis. Interestingly, the first Levi Jeans were made from hemp. Until late nineteenth century hemp remained an invaluable cash crop for farmers in Canada. Later, with American cotton becoming cheaper every year, farmers began to abandon this labour-intensive crop. Then in 1938, the Canadian government outlawed growing of hemp since it contained small percentage of narcotic contents that is found in a drug named Marijuana. Since the Second World War, the main areas of fibre hemp production have been China, the former Soviet Union and Eastern Europe.

Now, in March 1998, after a gap of 60 years Government of Canada once again allowed growing of Hemp since the narcotic contents of Hemp are found to be minuscule and of little harm. Hemp plant is environmentally friendly since its production requires no pesticide applications due to its extraordinary ability to suppress weeds. The plant is quick to mature, requiring between 90 and 110 days from planting to harvesting. Its deep roots help improve soil structure, and as much as 60 per cent of the nutrient, which hemp takes from the ground, are returned to the ground. Other than textile uses hemp is used in construction materials, cosmetics, paints, papers and fibreboard. There is a good market for hemp products. It is estimated that the current market for Hemp in North America is between $28 and $30 million a year and it is apparently increasing at the rate of $8 to $10 million annually. Indian research institutions connected with bast fibres should explore the possibilities of plantation of Hemp in India in a big way.

Developmental constraints

Developments of mechanised methods of yarn production from Bast fibres dates back to the beginning of nineteenth century. The spinning system includes hackled flax, tow and jute system. There are two main constraints in the developments of bast fibre. Those are low levels of fibre yield and difficulties in retting process. Further in most of the jute mills in India the technology of fibre processing and yarn manufacturing has become outdated. In ITMA'99 at least six renowned long fibre machine manufacturers exhibited latest models of spinning and processing machinery. Institutions like International Jute Organisation and British Textile Technology Group have taken the initiative to develop new production processes for Jute, particularly one based on Non-woven.

Researchers in USA and Canada are concentrating on cost-effective methods for the fibre cultivation and retting of bast fibres using biotechnology. In India we should explore the possibility of cultivating bast fibres other than Jute and develop their finer varieties. Further in order to sustain consistent growth of ecofibres, Indian jute industry need to invest in newer technologies both for cultivation and processing of bast fibres. In this regard Technology Upgradation Fund is a timely incentive for bast fibres industries.

Chapter 12

Fibres; Luxurious and Warm

Other than wool, there are varieties of animal hairs, which are source of textile material. Garments made out of these animal hairs are luxurious, warmer, softer, and highly priced. Shawls made from Shahtoosh and Pashmina, which could pass through a ring, were exported to Europe. For ages, European marvelled at these products. Regrettably, India could not preserve the advantage of its textile heritage. Over the years, we lost not only this lucrative trade, the peerless artisans but in some case, the original breed of these fibre-provider animals.

Contrary to this, in foreign countries, they nurture various animals for their fibres. These fibre-providers mainly belong to three principal animal sources, rabbit, goat, and camel families. The goat (Capra hircus), along with sheep, were among the earliest domesticated fibre-providers. Other than these, there are fur-provider animals, such as Vair, Nutria, Muskrat, Fox, Beaver, Raccoon and Weasel, mostly found in Europe and America. The fur of these animals is beautiful, silky and most valuable textile material. There are even some breeds of dog, whose hairs make exclusive winter clothes. In USA, they spin small quantities of these fibres by using a drop spindle (Takli).

Pashmina and Shahtoosh

In Kashmir, they still have a tradition of rearing Pashmina goats and make beautiful shawls from its hairs for domestic sales and exports. In winters, one can see Kashmiri hawkers going around places to sell their products and earn a handsome amount on their sales. Lately, some unscrupulous traders have also entered in this business and they try to sell spurious products. Traditionally, Kashmiri people spin these fibres on hand wheels (charkha) and knit manually or weave on handlooms in their tiny and cottage industries.

Cashmere, as the world knows this royal fibre, came from Kashmir goats. Later Englishmen exported some Pashmina goats to Europe, where they thrived but subjected to crossbreeding. Cashmere wool derived its name from these Kashmiri goats. Pashmina as they call this wool in India is simply the best cashmere in the world. Those who have experienced the sheer lightness, softness and warmth of an original Pashmina wrap hardly look twice at cashmere.

Shahtoosh, the fiber of the Gods, as they call it is the rarest of animal fibre and comes from an antelope, Chiru. It is much finer and warmer than cashmere. It takes months for a Shahtoosh shawl to be completed and then months more if the famous Kashmir embroidery is added. Some large blankets can take up to a year. Shahtoosh shawls were the prize treasures of the royal and wealthy families of India. The soaring commercial demand of these shawls has forced the Chiru onto the endangered species list.

Mohair

Mohair, a silky hair obtained from Angora goat derives its name from the Arabic 'mukhayar' which means "to choose" or "prefer." Mohair is very similar to wool in chemical composition but differs from wool on many accounts. It is the shiniest fibre amongst the animal hair category. In India, woollen industry imports mohair mainly from Texas. Kid mohair from Texas is the best quality in the world. This is because Kemp and modulated fibres contents in Texas mohair are less than 2 per cent.

Mohair fibre is valued for its flame-resistance, and high sound absorbency for making decorative and upholstering fabrics. In Ludhiana, they blend 30 per cent kid mohair with acrylic and make boucle yarns on fancy twister with polyester filament wrapping. Further, these yarns are brushed to make them hairy. They export sweaters made of this yarn to Russia in bulk.

Alpaca and Llama

Llama, Alpaca, Guanaco and the Vicuna belong to camelid family. Guanaco and the Vicuna are wild animals and are on the endangered list. Both have extremely fine fiber and make the softest coat clothe in the world. The llama and the alpaca are both domesticated animals, and have never been wild. They are native to South America, specifically the Andes regions of Peru and Chile. The fibres of these animals are lightweight warm, silky and luxurious to handle, incredible lustrous that could make finest textiles. These fibres are available in white, light brown and black shades.

True alpaca is expensive so often combined with other fibres. These fibres find its uses in men and women coats, elegant evening gowns, sportswear, linings and sweaters. This coupled with their fleece being practically greaseless, means that people who are allergic to wool can comfortably wear garments made of camel hairs.

Angora

Angora fibre is the hair of angora rabbits. One should not confuse this with Angora goat the provider of mohair. The angora fibre is eight times warmer than sheep wool and provides warmth without weight. The popular breeds of angora rabbits are French Angoras, Giant Angoras, Satin Angoras and English Angoras. They harvest angora fibre during the natural shedding process of Rabbits.

Nature provides Angora rabbit with a coat that sheds periodically. No harm comes to angora rabbits during harvesting. Average life of Angora rabbit is four years. Angora fibres are often blended and mixed with wool to lower the price of the finished article or to obtain fancy or novelty effects. Ludhiana knitwear manufacturers make beautiful sweaters from imported angora blended with wool and nylon.

Conclusion

Other than sheep and famous Pashmina goats, there is no tradition for breeding fibre-provider animals in India. Since long, Indian scientists have made efforts to develop apparel grade sheep wool, but these efforts have not brought any perceptible results. Also some private small enterprises in the semi-hilly areas of Himachal and Uttar Pradesh made efforts to breed angora rabbits. Climate of these places is conducive for rabbit breeding. However, quantities produced of angora wool are yet insignificant and quality not comparable with imported angora. Growers need the support of the government and financial Institutions to establish good rabbitry farms. Somewhat labour intensive to care for, angora rabbits are rewarding to work with. In South-America, there are many breeder associations, which register, breed, and standardise these fibre-provider animals on organised and scientific basis.

Further, there is an ongoing controversy regarding use of Shahtoosh products. Some people believe that Shahtoosh-provider antelope, Chiru, shed its hair twice a year, rubbing their fleeces against rocks or bushes. Wind blows their hair into little clumps. Kashmiri, Tibetans and Nepalese trek through the mountains for weeks in search of Shahtoosh and return with only handfuls of wool. Others believe that they kill the animals to obtain hairs and want ban on the sale of Shahtoosh products to continue. If that were so, the Chiru must be extinct by now, argue Kashmiri traders. Their argument deserves some merit. Government of J & K must dig out the truth for the sake of this fibre royal, the warmest amongst the textile fibres.

Chapter 13
Wool Marketing Mechanism

India imports its entire requirement of apparel grade raw wool mainly from Australia. The country consumes approximately 2 per cent of the global output. According to a forecast made by International Wool Secretariat the consumption of apparel grade wool in India will increase by 200 per cent from its present level of 26 million by the year 2005. Australia, New Zealand and South Africa collectively supply over 50 per cent of the world's requirements of all grades of wool including merino, lambs and coarse wool. The developing countries relatively supply only a small quantity. Australia alone is world's major source of fine merino wool, supplying over 70% of the global requirement. Most of the merino wool is used for the manufacturing of apparel garments such as suits, knitwear and skirts. In most cases, therefore, if a developing country wanted to go heavily into woollen production, the raw material will have to be imported.

As published by Australian Wool Exporters Council, there are approximately 160 million sheep in Australia that produce more than one quarter of the world's total wool. Australia exports over 95% of its wool production, generating about $US 2.1 billion in export earnings. In order to make wool marketing efficient and cost effective Australia now makes use of information technology. Ironically, in the second half of nineties the Australian wool industry passed through a crisis due to global recession and stockpiles.

Marketing Mechanism

There are many marketing options available to the woolgrowers in Australia. These are Public Auction, Public Tender, and Private Treaty. There are three major selling centres in Australia, Freemantle (Western Australia), Melbourne (Victoria) and Sydney (New South Wales). Selling by Public Auction is the preferred method adopted by the woolgrowers.

In this method, woolgrowers offer their wool for sale, through their Wool brokers, at public auction to the highest bidder.

Several days prior to the auctioning, Woolbroker display grab samples in boxes for the buyers to appraise. These boxes are numbered and arranged on the show floor of a display room. Each Woolbroker publishes catalogue listing the wool under their control for sale. The catalogue contains relevant details of all the samples displayed. The details include test results of the fibre diameter, yield and vegetable matter content, and if requested by the grower, some additional measurements such as staple length, staple strength and point of break are also listed. Australian Wool Testing Laboratory or other testing organisations issues the test certificates.

Wool brokers conduct the auction under the auspices of the 'National Council of Wool Selling Brokers' of Australia. The auction rooms, within each selling centre, are located at a place separate to the display show floor. The wool buyers who constitute exporters, representatives of foreign buying houses and Mills, attend these auctions. These buyers compete with each other in the auction system known as "open cry" or 'progressive bidding" system. One particular Wool broker is in control of auction at a particular time.

The auction results are progressively made public, which subsequently enables quick and up-to-date market reporting of values of each type or description of the wool. Specialised skills are required for a buyer's representative to partake in the auction due to speed of auctioning, coupled with keen and wide-spread buying competition, which result in hectic conditions in the auction room

In Public tender method of selling, they link a computer system to telex or fax which accept bids for lines of wool samples displayed. When tenders are closed, computer determines the highest bidder who receives the advice on the telex. In the alternative option, i.e., Private Treaty method of selling, the woolgrower negotiate a sale direct with the wool merchants. By this method the woolgrower gets ready payment for his wool clips. Private merchants in turn dispose off clips by traditional methods, where they display number of bales depending on the lot size. Here the buyers appraise the wool through subjective methods only.

The auction system is the best vehicle to market growers wool. In 1996-97, Australia sold 84 per cent of the wool through auction system.

Each consignment of wool sold is accompanied by a presale test certificate issued by Australian Wool Testing Authority Ltd. (AWTA Ltd.), which contains the measurements of mean fibre diameter, vegetable matter and various commercial yields. Ranges of vegetable matters and fibre diameter between the individual lots are also printed on the certificates. In order to facilitate combining individual sale lots to form a processing consignment, a 'combined certificate' is issued, which specify the method of combination of the yield and fineness component of the lots by an IWTO standard. If required the additional measurements of staple length and strength are also included in the certificates.

Electronic Selling

In the nineties most of the development had occurred in the area of electronic selling. The rapid growth of information technology enabled the handling and selling of wool entirely by electronic system. Now they took number of steps to improve the efficiency of wool selling and buying by auction. In the electronic system there is a rapid flow of information from the time of clipping and growers classifications for onward transmission. The broker or handling agent usually electronically sends all bale details; brands, weights, etc to the testing authority. After the samples have been drawn and tested, the testing authority electronically transmits all the test results to the broker or handling agent. At this stage the broker collates the information and prepares an electronic catalogue for transmission to exporters.

Registered buyers access the electronic catalogue on Internet. Now it is the ability of the exporter or other buyer's representatives to match the information in the catalogue with the requirements of their Mill. They transmit their evaluation to the mills anywhere in the world, and the mills in turn send to the exporter or their representatives the limits/orders based on data received. The buyers also have the option to connect their computers direct to the sale room computer. They may submit bids on forthcoming lots and improve the calling price thereby reducing selling times. Updated weekly information on the price trend in the auction is also available on the Internet. This has enabled cost efficient means of accessing a wider range of wool on offer for sale by any method, by auction, private treaty or forward selling.

Some woolgrowers prefer to sell through 'futures'. They obtain quotations for forward months and may like to sell taking advantage of currently prevalent high prices. Futures are sold now instead of wool and bought back at the time of delivery of wool. Any fall in the price of the wool is compensated for by the fact that futures are then cheaper to buy back. A profit on the futures tends to out-weigh a loss on the wool sold. Apart for providing insurance, futures can make planning and budgeting more certain. Electronic forms for quoting wool are accessible on the Internet.

Distribution and Transportation

After the wool has been bought at auction, the buyer's shipping instructions are issued via the wool delivery order to the shipping company, who in turn instruct the selling broker to deliver the buyer's purchases for commencement of shipping preparation. By far the most prevalent method of preparing bales for shipment is by dumping. This economic stowage of wool for shipment overseas has not really changed for many years. Dumping of the bales into normal, high, or super density to reduce the size of the bale, thus more number of bales could be accommodated in the containers. Depending upon the density and number of bands used, a 6.1 meters container can accommodate between 63 (normal), and 80 (high), 100 (super) single dumped bales.

The other form of 'super-density' packaging now rapidly becoming popular for exporting Australian wool is the three-bale compactor or tri-pack. This development has opened new frontiers for the packaging of wool for overseas export. In this method, three bales are compressed and compacted, end to end, into a single 'super density' module. Tri-pack weighs between 450 and 600 kilos and its dimensions measure only fractionally more then a conventional farm bale. Tri-pack has achieved container payloads between 17 and 21 tonnes, comprising up to 108 farm bales in a 20 feet container.

Chapter 14

Wool; A Perception

Previously Australian Wool Corporation (AWC), a statutory authority now disbanded, regulated a reserve price scheme or floor prices of wool. Under these schemes, the AWC would buy all wool offered for sale, which did not attract bids from other buyers at or above the AWC reserve prices at auction. The minimum reserve price pronounced at the beginning of July each year remained in force for a period of twelve months. As published in their bulletin, the then Australian Wool Corporation used to determine the minimum price, after a thorough evaluation of the prevailing conditions, in the wool textile industry through out the world. They based the prices on the highest sustainable price level consistent with the long-term trends in the wool textile industry. In addition, emphasis was on levels of consumption in the manufacturing sector as well as movements in world currencies.

In 1989-90, the production at 1170 million kilos of clean wool, was a peak in five major wool exporting countries, they are, Australia, New Zealand, South Africa, Argentina and Uruguay. This coupled with decrease in global wool demand made prices to crash, consequently, the stock of raw wool piled up with the AWC. Thereafter, they abandoned the reserve price scheme and left it to market forces to decide the wool prices. In 1992-93, average raw wool prices were a record low to 480 Australian cents a kilo clean. They ascribed this to the recession that engulfed the major wool consuming countries, that is, China, Japan, Western Europe and USA. There was trade restrictions in China, structural changes taking place within the Japanese textile industry, and slow global economic growth and high unemployment in Europe.

Simultaneously, the production of wool also fell, and as per estimates, the fall in the production during 1997-98 year was to the extent of 35 per cent from the 1989-90 peak in the five major exporting countries. Now, if required, they met the difference in demand and production from the stockpile of wool held by Australian Government and that of the private woolgrowers. This checked the wool prices to the detriment of woolgrowers for which the wool farming no longer remained a lucrative business. As per a report, Australian Government even considered freezing the sales from the stockpile to overcome the prevalent crises at that time in the Australian wool industry.

Perspective

The global output of wool more or less has been static. One factor to consider is that the consumption of wool as fibre compared with other fibres is diminishing. Till the end of the millennium the share of wool in the world's fibre demand was less than 5 per cent. The average growth rate of wool has been projected at 1.5 per cent as compared to 4.1 per cent of the synthetics. More than this, all indications are that man-made fibres will continue to penetration increasingly in the global market at the expense of natural fibres.

In coming times wool is likely to face a tough competition from man-made fibres. However, International Wool Secretariat opined that the consumption of wool in India would increase because younger consumer was increasingly showing its preference to the woollen ready-mades. Moreover, they see a bright future for wool consumption in India due to exports of textiles being the thirst area of the Indian Government.

However, declining wool production and freezing the releases from the stockpile could result in further contraction in wool availability resulting in increase in prices. This was also likely to challenge the long-term viability of the wool producing industries that was already passing under lean period. More so for wool combers, whose functioning, for example, is entirely dependent on wool supply. Also the worsted spinners, although they can use other long fibres, consume predominantly wool top. And the short staple woollen spinning sector is more prices sensitive, more subject to shifts in consumer tastes and receives hardly any technical support. Therefore factors that ultimately would determine the off-take of wool, are level and stability of comparative fibre prices and availability of fibres when required.

To make matters worse, the customers are not dependent entirely on wool. In case of non-availability of wool, they have a choice to other fibre types and blends, such as polyester/wool, viscose/wool, wool/silk, polyester/viscose and acrylics. One thing positive for wool is that the worsted and woollen spinning sectors have an interest in continuing supplies of wool, although they are able to adjust progressively to alternative fibre supplies.

IWS published a broad estimate of the ratio between average wool prices and corresponding synthetic fibre prices, both globally and by region. Some experts' feel that, supply factors aside, a ratio above 3.0 is not sustainable in the long-term. However, in June '97 this ratio was high at 4. IWS concluded that three factors, that is, rising wool prices, a strong $A and declining prices of man-made fibres contributed to a rise in the global ratio of wool to synthetic fibres. Subsequently, aided by a much lower $A, the ratio had declined to 3.5 by late 1997.

Product Innovation

Indian market has vast, yet untapped, potential for wool consumption both for domestic end uses and for exports. One significant factor, which favours wool, is its image as warm and natural fibre with a traditional place in men and women's apparel. Agencies engaged in wool development should preserve the advantage for wool conveyed by that image along with its other natural attributes. Moreover, woollen goods are normally associated with fashion items more than cotton and man-made fibres. Product innovation and development of new yarns and fabrics is important and critical for wool to survive in this increasingly selective consumer market.

Some new products developed by IWS are exportable and also worth a trial in Indian market. These products are Wool/Lycra active wear, undergarments, and shrink proofed machine washable knitwear, Wool/Supriva mix lightweight fabric for garments with improved fluidity and drapes. Further to that, a technology has been developed to treat wool chemically to make it stretch and feel like cashmere. The new technology to weave singles of bi-component spun yarns makes good fabrics for lightweight jackets, sweaters and trousers. Strategically, promoting 'Woolblendmark' by IWS in Indian market may become the best bet. Besides, apparel sector has yet to exploit wide-open area of high potential casual wear such as shirts, skirts, and now jeans made of cots-wool. One may find that the differences between the "worsted" and "woollen" and "cotton" primary textile industries are becoming less distinct. International Wool Secretariat, now renamed as The Woolmark Company, has a job in hand to perform in India.

Chapter 15

The Traditional Silk Industry

The story of origin of silk is interesting. It was only a chance that a cocoon fell into the steaming tea bowl of wife of a Chinese emperor while she was enjoying her tea in the garden underneath a mulberry tree. The act of taking out the cocoon from the hot bowl led to reeling off lustrous filaments. This is how silk and its production technology was discovered in 2640 BC.

Even today cultivated silk live on mulberry leaves and its cocoons are softened in hot water to remove the gum called sericin, which surrounds them thus freeing silk filaments for reeling. For some 3,000 years Chinese closely guarded the secret of silk production to the extent that punishment for smuggling eggs and cocoons out of China was death. However, shortly after 300 AD, as the legend goes, it was left to the grit and fortitude of a Chinese princess married to an Indian prince, who brought the eggs of silkworm and seeds of mulberry tree to India concealed in her head-dress.

Thus sericulture, the silk production technique, got established in India. The mass silk production method today is a blend of ancient techniques and modern innovations. From India the silk industry spread into Persia and Central Asia, then slowly filtered into the Mediterranean countries. Sericulture also reached Japan through Korea, but not before the early part of the third century. Beginning early in the 2nd century BC, caravans travelled the Silk Road, a 4,000-mile trade route linking China with the West and wound its way to the countries along the eastern Mediterranean shores.

The Silk Road allowed a highly lucrative trade in silk fabrics to develop. Presently silk is produced in 35 countries around the world including many European countries including France and Italy. However, the silk industry did not flourish everywhere. India, though the leading consumer of silk fibre is the second largest producer of raw silk next only to China. Other major silk producing countries include Japan and Brazil.

Sericulture Base

The estimated global production of raw silk is about 9000 metric tonnes. Apart from mulberry silk, which is a cultivated variety, there are Tasser, Eri, and Muga silk varieties, which are wild silk since these grow in the forests. India is the only country, which produces all the four varieties of silk with 92% share of the mulberry silk. There are 60 Lakh family units that are dependent on silk industry in India. Major centres of mulberry sericulture in India are Karnataka, Andhra Pradesh, Tamil Nadu, West Bengal and Jammu and Kashmir. The major silk weaving centres in the country are Bhagalpur, Varanasi, and Banglore.

Since ancient times silk textiles formed an essential component of Indian festivities and marriage ceremonies. The domestic demand of silk textiles fluctuates with the number and fervour of these occasions. Thus India will continue to have strong domestic base for silk products. In the year 1997-98, out of 270 million meters of fabric produced in the country only 15 per cent of this were exported with value additionand the balance consumed in the domestic market.

Presently in India, demand of silk raw materials has been projected at 24,000 MT, whereas the production of raw silk in the country has touched only 15,190 MT in the year 1997-98. In order to meet this gap in the demand and supply government allowed import of silk against special import licence, in addition to duty free imports against exports obligation. In an estimate it was found that almost 32 per cent of the raw silk demand in the country is being met through imports including smuggled routes.

Interestingly, only 40 per cent of the imported silk are consumed to meet the export demand. Another reason for imports of raw silk is the quality of the Indian raw silk, which is not viable for using as warp on the powerlooms. Chinese silk has been found to be superior in this respect. However, these imports have affected the domestic industry since imported silk is not only of good quality but also cheaper by Rs 400 per Kilo. These imports forced the domestic supplier to lower their prices. The growers of cocoons were also said to be discouraged as ultimately they were also forced to lower prices by Rs 20 to 30. That washed away their already meagre profit margins.

In the year 1998-99, India exported silk textiles worth Rs. 1053.57 crores, which is only 2 per cent share in the total textile exports from India. At present the gap between the value of goods exported and that of raw silk imported is narrow and keeps oscillating in favour and against of imports now and than. Therefore, in the ultimate analysis it is essential that we strengthen and broaden our own sericulture base, bring down the cost of production, and improve the quality of raw silk to posses competitive edge in the global market.

Quality and Productivity

Presently, China produces about 500,000 metric tonnes of Cocoons. With approx. 143 grams of reelable raw silk yield per 1 kilo of cocoons it produces 71500 kilos of raw silk, which is almost 80 per cent of the global production. In India the average yield of raw silk per kilo of cocoons, over the years, has been more or less 110 grams. Even in Brazil the raw silk yield is 152 grams per kilo cocoons. During upsurge in the Japanese silk Industry the yield per kilo of cocoons was about 200 grams, and per hectare of land under sericulture yielded more than 600 kilos of raw silk against a yield of 440 kilos at present in India. Obviously there is much scope of improvement both in yield and quality of raw silk in the Indian sericulture industry.

In this context Japan has extended a helping hand to improve the much-required yield and quality of cocoons and silk yarn produced in India under an Indo-Japan joint project. Under these projects bivoltine silkworms have been reared instead of traditional multivoltine ones and the Japanese stand to pass on the necessary technology and training to our Sericulturists. Bivoltine silkworms rear two generations in a year and multivoltine many times in a year. But the quality of silk produced from bivoltine silkworms is superior and can be used as warp on powerlooms. It was encouraging to note that the results of bivoltine rearing even in Kerala, a non-traditional silk rearing centre, were very encouraging and the rearing cost have come down considerably.

Now farmers at various centres are encouraged to rear superior variety of bivoltine silkworms. Further, the central Silk Board, a statutory organisation responsible for implementing the development schemes in sericulture is making all out R & D efforts to develop superior technologies for silkworm rearing to improve the quality and productivity. Under the ninth plan, the textile ministry has envisaged an increase in the production of mulberry raw silk by 6000 tonnes and that of non-mulberry silk by 540 tonnes through these R & D efforts. This may change the Indian silk scenario in the present millennium.

Research in Silk

Experts feel that it is necessary to create economically viable silk production techniques in order to meet wider objectives. In line with this the out come of many researches conducted at various silk-producing centres of the world aimed at improving the quality and productivity, besides alternative uses of silk. Some of these researches have been explored commercially also.

Scientist of Central Sericulture Research and Training Institute, Mysore developed a multipurpose disinfectant which can protect the silkworms against any disease, thereby increasing the possibility of increasing the yield per laying by 10 to 15 kilogram per 100 disease free laying (DFLs). Previously 20 to 40 per cent of the silk crop was lost due to diseases. The textile division of IIT-Delhi developed a silk degumming technique by the use of enzymes, which improves the lustre of silk filament. Lately researchers have found the use of silk fibres in bio-medical and biotechnological applications due to its excellent resistance to biological attacks and good biological compatibility.

The Department of Bio-technology, government of India is handling a project jointly with a French scientific agency to study the genome of the silkworm 'bombyx mori' in its pursuit to improve quality and productivity of silk. The outcome of such research efforts should be immediately transferred from laboratory to the field for the silk industry to accrue benefits.

'SilkMark'

Over the years the good image of silk has received a set back. One of the reasons has been development of imitations of silk with rayon and synthetics. The manufactured fibres have even penetrated into the domain of traditional silk fabrics like Brocades, Chiffon, Organza, Georgette, Satin and Taffeta. There is considerable price difference between silks and its imitations. In the absence of any trademark for genuine silk, consumers at large find themselves cheated on many occasions. Recently there have been some cases referred to consumer protection courts where 'genuine silk' sarees gifted as dowry turned out to be an imitation, to the utter disgust of the dower who spent fortunes to make daughter's dowry. There is hardly any national or international body to protect the interests of silk industry on the similar lines as they do in case of wool.

Recently the International Silk Association (ISA) has expressed concern over the fall in the demand for silk across the world and realised that the fall was on account of anomalies in silk marketing and absence of silk promotion. The ISA has stressed the need for promoting silk on similar lines of wool and if necessary, an additional levy might be included in the prices of all sales made by the producer of primary stages of raw silk. India being the largest consumer of silk should take the initiative to promote a 'SilkMark'. These steps are essential if Indian silk industry has to maintain its silken edge, simultaneously meeting the imposing challenge of China in the global silk market.

Chapter 16

Handlooms; The Heritage Industry

Handloom weaving symbolises the regional sartorial ethos of India. The contribution of handloom sector towards national economy as a whole and the textile sector in particular is considerable. This industry has the lowest investment per person employment and capital output ratio. Moreover, this industry makes little demand on the conventional sources of energy and had no ecological effects.

Handloom weaving is the largest economic activity in India after agriculture providing direct and indirect employment to more than 30 Lakh weavers' family units in rural and semi-urban areas. The official figures indicate that the production of handloom cloth in the country accounts approximately 23 per cent of total cloth production. The export of handloom cotton fabrics and made-ups worth Rs.1859 crores during 1997-98 was very significant. Recently, handloom sector has witnessed sustained onslaught from the mechanised textile sectors. Over and above, the global recession started in the second half of nineties had its toll on handloom sector also. In view of this, handloom sector, the heritage industry, needs a sustained government protection from further degradation.

Power of Tradition

From ancient times handlooms and silk are synonymous. One can relate the art of block printing, Patola, Tinsel and Ikat work, Jamdhani and Baluchuri silk brocades with handlooms. Varanasi is perhaps the oldest handloom centre for silk weaving in India. Samples of Varanasi silk brocades dating back to the seventeenth century are displayed in some museums and churches in Europe and Canada. Besides Uttar Pradesh, the other important handloom-centres of silk and cotton weaving are Chennai, Karnatka, Andhra Pradesh, W. Bengal, and Maharashtra.

In North Eeastern States, people still have the tradition to weave clothes, bridal wears and others for self-consumption. Even in Japan, a century ago, every household had at least one handloom. Young women learned weaving from their elders. Actually hand-woven textiles were a part of everyday life in Japan until the middle of this century. Besides Japan, the tradition of handloom weaving exists in Thailand and China. With an uncertain future, the Japanese weaving industry has been striving to combine present day technology with the power of traditional handloom weaving. Such a combination, they hoped, will allow new concepts in textiles, open new markets for the unique fabrics of Japan.

In India also many Weavers' Service Centres have resorted to computer aided designing for handloom fabrics. It is not only a matter of protecting this traditional weaving on handlooms, its ethnic sartorial culture and the artisans from becoming extinct. But the continuation of this industry is paramount from the point of view that there could not be any viable alternative source of high employment generation in the rural areas. Therefore, it is necessary that handlooms and the mechanised weaving industry go parallel to each other, each with its own characteristic fabric production. In this regard Government has done well by reserving some items for exclusive production on handlooms.

The Handloom Technology

Basic technology of handloom and powerloom weaving is the same that is interlacing of warp and weft with the only difference that one is a manual operation and the other runs with electric power. Even though handlooms could weave all type of fabrics, yet traditionally and historically the handloom weaving was confined to ethnic items like silk products and Khadi. Technically speaking, handloom weaving was an extraordinary ancient invention to weave intricate designs out of weaker and hand spun yarns of silk, cotton, wool and other animal fibres. Even now hand-spun yarns are unable to withstand the stresses and strains of the powerloom weaving and its preparatory processes. For instance recently to weave silk yarns viably on the powerlooms, manufacturers had to import/smuggle stronger silk yarns from China to be used as warp. On the other hand, to weave non-traditional items and that of strong synthetic yarns on handlooms is indeed a trespass on the territory of powerlooms.

During one of the assignments connected with the development of handlooms handled by the author in the early eighties, he noticed that in a small town of eastern U.P, improvised wooden framed handlooms were being run by 1/2 H.P. motors. At that time authorisation was required to install powerlooms. Therefore, in order to cover the visits of inspecting authorities, the weavers made the provision on those looms to remove the motors and other paraphernalia with in five minutes notice and than resume weaving by hands. The town is inhabited by one community and is known for weaving madras lungi on handlooms. This small town consumed about 50 tons of viscose filament yarns per month at that time, said to be on handlooms. But obviously the viability of weaving lungis and the delivery commitments were on power run looms.

In this regard there is some merit in the complaint of powerloom industry that the government have shown undue favour to the handloom industry by reserving some items of mass consumption like lungies and saris which has led to the closure of many powerloom units. Powerloom people also argue that the cost of lungies produced on the powerlooms is lesser as compared with handlooms. But if their suggestion also include the traditional saris made of cotton and silk than they, unwittingly, are attacking the legitimate and heritage right of the handlooms.

Until there is clarity and technical precision in the defining the terminology of items reserved for the handlooms, such a controversy would persist. There was opposition from the woollen mills on reserving the blankets for handlooms. Similarly one can understand weaving of shawls on handlooms made of animal fibres such as Pashmina, Angora and that of woollen system or handspun yarns, but to reserve shawls made from worsted yarns is out of place. Government will do well by revising items for the reservation of handloom taking into consideration traditional, technical, and viability factors.

Modernisation of Handlooms

It will be wrong to say that handloom industry should not have its share in the cake of the technology upgradation fund. The argument is that this industry being not mechanised has nothing to modernise. It is possible to modify pit looms, frame looms, semi automatic looms, and pedal looms. Modernisation program of these handlooms should aim at relieving the strain on the weavers as well as increasing the output and consistent quality from each loom. The improvements in the existing processes of winding, warping, and weaving and dyeing and finishing facilities would be different for a single loom unit in a village and those for handlooms working in the centalised place like factories. It is understood that the Indian Institutes of Handloom Technology at Varanasi and Salem has done some work in this respect.

As regards handlooms working in a centalised factory the improvements required are 'hank to cone' winding machines and pirn winder for weft yarns in place of Charkha winding. The advantages of winding cones at uniform tension will reduce faults in the warping process. For handlooms, both working in a village unit or centralised factories, the equipment and attachments recommended are healds with inset glass eyelets or twisted wire, evenly spaced smooth metallic reeds instead of bamboo, five or seven wheel or the worm wheel type take up motion. Use of roller temples, smooth sley boards preferably covered with plush fabrics for smooth passage of the shuttles, and glass or aluminium lease-rods instead of wood or bamboo. Rubber covered emery beams may be used for smooth passage of the fabric. Such handlooms are used in USA and Europe. Use of fur lined lightweight shuttles made of rose wood will eliminate yarn splitting and damage during weaving.

The Handloom Institutes should be entrusted with the task of working the cost of Modernisation of handlooms and the accessories, which may vary depending upon type and place. Further, the major difficulty faced by the handloom factories is the warp sizing. The traditional method of sizing is done in streets by stretching the warp in the open, applying the Ganji and brushing. During rainy season this operation is not possible. A hand-driven long length combined warping and sizing units developed by IIHTs may be used.

Distortions

One of the biggest problems, which the handloom industry have been facing, pertains to marketing the goods produced. This problem keeps persisting and has become a chronic feature of this industry. Stock piling of silk and cotton products in the southern handloom sector is one of the recent examples. Such things happen besides the fact that government has provided various market development assistance schemes, marketing outlets such as National Handloom Expos, International Trade Fairs, and the export marketing efforts of HHEPC. One of the factors of its poor marketing performance could be its being in the decentalised sector with little access to global market trends and consumer tastes. Where as the organised sector has ways and means for the marketing of their products through an excellent retail network, cost reduction and aggressive sales promotion. These marketing inadequacies of the handloom sector have accentuated in recent years with the modernisation of the organised textile sector and the authorisation of the powerlooms.

Until some concerted efforts are made on national level and some other export avenues are explored, the distortions in production and marketing may well usher in an era of handloom crises leading to large-scale unemployment. If all the important aspects of the handloom industry are carefully attended to, the industry can emerge as a modern, commercially viable, forward looking industry, which can hold its own against the mechanised textile industry in the present millennium.

Chapter 17

Developments in Manufactured Fibre Industry

Emerging technologies, volatility in the global economy, the upheaval in the South East Asian currencies, coupled with general industrial recession created turmoil at the market place. Generally, under such circumstances the most affected are the segments of industries, with over capacities, technological obsolescence, inflexible production lines, and with watered capital and cost sensitive structures. In this scenario, global man-made fibre industry is no exception and is already in the throes of depression. Mounting losses of some companies have forced shelving new project proposals and expansions plans. Prices of synthetics touched to all time low in 1998-99 and the recovery was not yet at sight. Somewhere they enforced anti-dumping duties and at other places anti-subsidy probes. Man-made fibre industry passed through a massive reshaping phase.

Restructuring

The major players who until now controlled textile fibre production worldwide are now retaining only profit yielding fields along with inevitable downsizing. For instance, reportedly, DuPont Co, the largest man-made fibre producer decided to shut down two of its cost impaired production lines of polyester filament yarn. Similarly, the Austrian Fibres company, Lenzing, underwent an arduous exercise to make its operations cost effective to improve its bottom-line. Akzo Nobel, Netherlands based chemical giant acquired the U.K. based Courtaulds business. Their new fibre business called Acordis have set its priorities to establish a cost efficient structure by consolidating its resources, both functionally and geographically.

In India also many synthetic producing companies are in the process of closing down, some caught in the worst financial quagmire. Some big domestic players have reported losses and others have curtailed their production. Leading producers are now contemplating upon strategic issues such as location of manufacturing plants, capacity levels, apart from restructuring the company composition.

Meeting the Challenge

Sale or restructuring of so many fibre businesses is not the only indication of the challenges, which continue to face the man-made fibres industry. On top of all this, the developments in natural textiles such as shrink-proof, wrinkle-free, soil-resistant, stain-resistant, and flame-resistant cotton fabrics threaten to make inroads in the domain of man-made fibres. Nonetheless, the picture of man-made textiles is not that dismal despite a drifting trend towards natural fibres in some fashion applications. One factor that has helped synthetics to maintain its supreme position is the research and development in newer areas. This provided the possibilities to engineer the man-made products comparable to natural textiles in its core properties, such as breathability and moisture transportation.

As if that was not sufficient, the producers of man-made fibres have gone a step higher by creating anti-bacterial and anti-allergic fibres, besides producing fibres with properties such as thermal-regulation, stretch for comfort and personal safety factors. Furthermore, technology has also helped creating a new branch of technical textiles, such as geotextiles, medical, industrial and other novel application of man-made fibres. All this has kept the dominance of man-made fibres over cotton, wool, and other plant fibres on consumption levels.

Consistent Growth

As the indication were the share of man-made fibres in the overall global output of all textile fibres continues to grow. According to CIRFS, the Brussels-based International Rayon and Synthetic Fibres Committee, man-made fibre production in 1997 reached a new record total of 27.5 million tons, which was 9 per cent higher than the level in 1996. Man-made fibre now accounts for 56 per cent out of total world production of 48.8 million tons of textile fibres. The consumption levels of raw cotton are 19.8 million tons (41%), and raw wool 1.4 million tons (3%) out of the total.

Output in the Asian countries have been more sharper as compared with Europe, China being on the top with output of 4.1 million tons in 1997, 10% higher over 1996 levels. This was greater than that of the entire EU with 3.6 million tons. But USA with 4.5 million tons of production surpassed all. One thing is obvious that the changes that are taking place in this industry are entirely market driven. Fibre producers are now entering highly specialised and more specific, functional and demanding fibre applications.

Innovative Fibres

New breeds of high performance man-made fibres are coming on the scene relegating the use of stereotypes. Today consumer expects so much from the apparel they wear that an alert fiber producer has to constantly research new ways to be in tandem with consumer expectations. Now there are synthetic fibres made of 'Phase Change Materials' that automatically adjust to the climate, keeping warm in the winter and cool in the summer. The all-season multi-functional outfits made of these fibres will keep the demand high in sports related fashion clothing. Moreover as per a market survey, a sporting and casual appearance is in vogue rather than only a sports requirement.

Further, there are garment made of synthetic materials that combine the properties of wind-proofing, extreme breathability, effective sweat management, and easy care properties. Hollow core polyester fibers made by DuPont that trap air inside the fiber, keeping the body warm is one such example. These fibers also move moisture away from the skin and evaporate into the air, so one stays dry and comfortable. The applications of these fibres are in active wear, shirts, tops, pants, underwear, hosiery, gloves, and hats. Further Wellman Inc has developed one synthetic fibre that provides comfort equivalent to natural fibre. The company claims that the fibre breathes and transports moisture through wicking action to the outer layer. In addition the fibre provides superb pill resistance, maintains excellent shape retention, and doesn't shrink, wrinkle or stretch.

Then there are micro-fibres finer than silk and now nanofibres with 1-micrometer diameter produced on experimental equipment at UMIST, Manchester. These fibres provide great covering power with low weight for protective clothing. Besides providing protection against vagaries of weather, wind, and fire, the producers have developed fibres that provide personal safety. For instance Kevlar, an aramid fiber produced by DuPont is flame-resistant. Further Akzo Nobel has developed fibres by incorporating certain pigments which both reflects and absorbs the Ultra Violet light thus avoiding the risk of skin ageing in areas with ozone depletion layers.

Intense Competition

In order to meet the increased demand for small batches of dope-dyed lots of these next generation fibres, producers have developed systems with maximum flexibility to spin even a 2-ton lot with minimum waste and change over time. This is in consonance with the evolving mass customisation concept. Barmag AG has developed such a system called Maflex. As reported this has also resulted in increased productivity and reduced environmental waste.

India has hardly any R&D base or infrastructure of its own for developing newer man-made fibres. Therefore, it has to depend upon technology transfer from advanced countries. Compared to the huge cost of R&D, which normally would be involved for researching new polymers or their extrusion technology, the route of importation of the technology may be a viable alternative. However, fibre producers in India always lagged behind in importing and adopting innovative technologies developed elsewhere in the world. In the near future yarn spinning mills in India will have a choice to import smaller lots of the speciality fibres to cater to the changing demands of the consumers, thereby making a dent in the indigenous fibre market. Presently, Indian man-made fibre industry needs innovations and consolidation rather than expansion to meet the intense competition, which awaits it in the 21st century.

Chapter 18

Cyberspace: Information Galore for Textile Researchers

Internet has changed the way of life of corporate world in developed countries. This will soon affect Indian corporate world in the similar fashion as fax machine and PC has. It has broken the walls between buyer and seller; manufacturer and retailer; institutions and industry, organisations and beneficiaries and even between nations, that has defined industrial developments and businesses since the Renaissance. Today, the global network is directly available to users, that is, researchers, engineering and manufacturing industries, and marketers. Now researchers located at remote distances can interchange data instantaneously. This eliminates wastage of time, money, and resources. Now, the manufacturer is taking over the stockroom and warehouse functions, to create just-in-time stocking.

The technology package behind this new kind of business arrangement includes electronic mail, electronic data interchange and electronic funds transfer. Information and knowledge is no longer captive. Experts feel that in ensuing years these technologies will find acceptance in most industries, organisations and universities. This culture will soon enter textile sector of India, leaving those companies and institutions behind that have not kept up pace with this fast changing world.

Enumerated below are some of the web sites, which one can surf using the power of Internet.

The Textile Institute

The Institute, based at Manchester (www.texi.org) was founded in 1910 and granted a Royal Charter in 1925, enabling it to award professional qualifications recognised worldwide. The mission of this Institute (TI) is to promote professionalism in all areas associated with the textile industries worldwide. Now with more than 7000 members, this institute has become a unique professional association for people working with fibres and fabrics, clothing and footwear, interior and technical textiles. The Textile Institute provides a comprehensive information, to its members and the public, on manufacturers, products, engineering applications, fashion design, technology and retailing, standards, terms and definitions and other information

The web site of the institution provides detailed information and useful links to various universities, research organisations, fibre manufacturers, and clothing associations of the world. From web surfing one could find the details of a project, which The Textile Institute had undertaken with a European Community to disseminate new quality control technology. The new technology envisages the application of High Performance Computing Network technology (HCPN) using image processing for product inspection and quality control.

Textile Web

Textile Web (www.textileweb.com) is a comprehensive site for links to almost all topics on textiles, commercial, technical and educational. A list of contents is available on its home page displaying fibres, yarns, textiles, machinery, apparel and accessories click buttons. One can reach to areas of interest by clicking the respective button. The featured site on the home page was Apparel Textile and Home Furnishings Industries. Textile Equipment site is for searching brand new, used and reconditioned textile machinery, parts, accessories, CAD equipment, manufacturer's representatives, and dealers. A link provides a complete list of textile manufacturers and facilities throughout the world. Fabric Link is an educational resource and a communication link developed for the textile, apparel, and retail industry and its consumers.

One can also visit directly to Davisons Textile Gold Book (www.apparelex.com/goldbook). This web site provides link to textile companies in the United States, Mexico, and Canada. Besides, it links you to directories of various countries for textile manufacturing equipment including Indian Textile Directory. The Korea Textile Communication (www.texcom.co.kr), a site resource for Korean textile companies, trading of textile, apparel, and garment. The Taiwan Textile Web (www.textiles.org.tw) represents Taiwan textile industries ranging from up-stream man-made fiber manufacturing to down-stream garment making.

Electronic Textiles

Textile Room (www.texnet.it) is another interesting web site. It gives various information regarding fibre content labelling, care labelling, basic 'textile weaves', and technical and commercial information and contains a textile dictionary. This dictionary converts textile words from Italian, French, Deutsche to English and vice-versa so don't be perturbed if you encounter some Italian words. It converted acrylic as "acrilico" in Italian. This site also leads you to commercial and technical web pages of Italy. Further, this page opens a web site Textile World, said to be the largest professional search index for textile raw materials, yarns, fabrics and machinery. The 'sample service' of this page provides a complete visualisation of archive, and TexChat, a real time chat that links you with textile operators. One can also look for calendar for important world textile exhibitions.

You may also register your company as agents, clients or a supplier in the Electronic Textiles link of this site. It provides you various contacts for your business. One of the informations contained on this web page is regarding label for fibre contents, and an awareness programme to textile consumer. This page educates that fibres are identifiable by its generic name. A label must name the manufacturer, the country where processed or manufactured, and the generic names and percentages of all fibers in the product. In addition to generic names, there are hundreds of trade names or trademarks. A trade name or trademark is the word or symbol used by fiber producers to distinguish their products from the products of other manufacturers. For examples, polyester is the fiber or generic name, and Dacron is a company trademark for polyester; acrylic is the fiber or generic name, and Orlon is a company trademark for acrylic.

Textile Library

Institute of Textile Technology, USA, has well equipped textile library named Roger Milliken Textile Library. The library with 30,000 volumes and 400 periodicals focused at textiles, may be the largest and most comprehensive collections of textile information in the world. The institute provides Masters degree of Textile Technology and is engaged in advanced research in textile manufacturing. Library services are also available to public, the textile industry at large, besides students and faculty members of the institute. The library catalogue can be accessed on-line. One can visit this library through its web site, www.itt.edu.

The Institute has undertaken research in new areas as directed by the industry supporters of ITT. Among the current areas of research involvement are World Class Manufacturing Strategies, Non-Woven Manufacturing and Computer-Aided Manufacturing tools and development. Besides important topics of textiles, the research is also focussed on environmental controls and energy saving topics related to textiles. Some recent topics of interest are; Surfactant Toxicity and Removal, Efforts to Utilise Environmental Information for Plant Improvements, and Textile Industry Air Pollution.

Buzzwords for the millennium

Surfing through the net one can find interesting discussions on very important indicators for the sustenance of development of the textile industry. Volatility in economic climate, fast changing consumer needs, and emerging technology has provoked the existing pattern of manufacturing. Attention of the researchers is focused to identify consumer wants, needs and interests. Researchers are also involved in combining production strategies with up to date manufacturing and information technology. The textile industry has also received due attention by the researchers. Here the idea is to meet consumer desires with customised textile and apparel products. In this respect, researchers are making efforts to define and build a model encompassing consumers' interests and concerns with industry's potential to deliver the required. For example, there is a need to establish a relationship between consumer to components of apparel design including colour, fabric and pattern, style and detail. This may require investigation in the overall ambit of textile business, be it management style, manufacturing technology, processes involved, packaging, distribution, or delivery of products. Researchers are addressing all these problems. There is also a suggestion to reorganise the business system in context of fast emerging technology culture. All these activities create an agenda for the current millennium.

Chapter 19

Moving Out Of Traditional Work Systems

Task-oriented jobs in today's hi-tech world are becoming obsolete. Instead, emerging concept is that companies must organise work around the processes involved. "Managers who understand and accept this concept of process-based work will help their companies leap ahead" as stated by Hammer and Champy, authors of the popular best seller 'Reengineering the Corporation'. The concept of reengineering a company means coming out of the shackles of conventional systems of managing production and businesses. It require radical redesign of business processes to achieve major gains in cost, service or time.

Technology is essentially a tool that provides the means. It has created new business pattern in a world where overnight delivery is no longer fast enough. Indeed, looking over the horizon it can be said that presently we are passing through a technology revolution. This revolution brings in a new model that redefines not only what we do, but also how we do it. The key to successful implementation of new technology and to reengineering in the rapidly changing global economy is in recognising the new, yet unknown capabilities of technology instead of its familiar ones. The crux of the concept is that change in work culture will change your results and the bottom line. Textile Industry of India, caught in the web of technology obsolescent, management apathy and financial quagmire urgently require to reengineer itself to come out of the sickness.

Demystifying ISO 9000 Standards

ISO 9000 standards are not the quality standards of the product. These standards are for a management system. The standards provide the organisation with a model to follow in setting up and operating the management system to ensure that the product meets the customer's requirements. The ISO technical committee approved the ISO 9000 standards. These standards encompass three quality assurance models against which an organisation can be certified. These are ISO 9001, ISO 9002 or ISO 9003. For an organisation that does not carry out design and development, ISO 9002 is the appropriate standard and ISO 9003 is the appropriate standard for those organisations, which use inspection and testing to ensure that final products and services meet specified requirements.

An organisation may choose its quality system for certification against ISO 9001, ISO 9002 or ISO 9003 according to their business processes. ISO 9000 family consists of more than 20 standards and guidelines. The auditing and certification are carried out independently of ISO by seperate certification bodies under their own responsibility. Textile industry of India needs to adopt ISO9000 standards to meet the export challenges in the post WTO regime.

ISO has published a handbook, ISO 9000 for Small Businesses (ISBN 92-67-10238-9), which dispels the myth that ISO 9000 is for big companies only. It provides guidance on all the three quality assurance models with clear explanations and many examples relevant to the small business. Experts from the Small Business Task Group of the ISO technical committee have written ISO 9000 for Small Businesses.

Computer Aided Management There has been sea change in the textile technology, management and information systems. Computers have entered almost all the departments of mill management. Be it production, administration, finance or marketing. One can not imagine 21st century without these computer packages. Earlier and even now in most of the textile mills, the process and quality control have been through mechanical means, gears, pulleys, gauges, hand wheels, manual inspections and analysis. These activities were mostly subjective and applied empirical methods for corrective actions. Moreover with conventional corrective methods there was always lag between occurrence of fault and corrective actions applied, and by that time 'much water flowed through the Ganges.'

Now, microcomputers based instruments built into the machines, specifically designed to suit all types of textile materials and machinery, are in use in the textile industry. These instruments, interface with host computers, are for measuring and displaying various pre-programmed parameters like length, production in hanks, speeds, delivery rate, and twist per inch. Some of these microprocessors and hybrid computers check and correct, actually on run-time. For example, microprocessor based yarn clearer and fault analysers on winders and auto-levellers for card and drawframes. Modern spinning mills may also use alarm for yarn faults and idle spindle and a data reporting on production efficiency at real time. Weaving dobby and jacquard fabrics by computer designing systems are other examples.

Similarly, microprocessors for dyeing, finishing and printing machines, computer control laboratory colour matching and dispensing equipment are emerging on the scene. CAD/CAM systems have revolutionised the garment technology. These programmable controllers are able to store, process data and control machines in a fully automatic way by limiting the intervention of the operator.

For mill management, packages are available for production planning, deciding product mix for maximising contribution depending upon availability of raw material and machinery as well as market potential. Actually all types of management information requirements, inventory, sales, budgetary, profitability and personnel, labour and machine productivity have been computerised. These packages run on PC and are on-line. The future lies in Computer Aided Management.

Technical Textiles

This non-traditional branch of textiles is now gaining ground. There still is an on-going debate to provide this sort of textiles a proper nomenclature. There are various terms used for 'technical textiles'. These are 'functional textiles', 'performance textiles", 'engineering textiles' and 'high-tech textiles'. One wonders what is there in a name. Then in what sense technical textiles are 'technical'? Most technical textiles are made from everyday polymers and materials such as polyester, polypropylene, polyamide, viscose, cotton, jute and even glass. Actually only a relatively small proportion of technical textiles uses the hi-tech fibres such as Aramids, Carbon fibres and high molecular weight Polyethylene.

The older definition of industrial textiles contained in the, 'Textile Terms and Definitions', a publication of The Textile Institute, is "textile materials and products intended for end-uses other than non-protective clothing, household, furnishing and floorcovering". The newer definition of technical textiles is "textile materials and products manufactured primarily for their technical performance" also deserves some consideration.

Very few, if any, comprehensive overviews of technical textiles exist in the book form. This industry at present is rather more focused than it once was before. Many of the companies manufacturing technical textiles no longer see themselves as textile producers but rather as manufacturers of car furnishings, filtration fabrics, surgical textiles etc. This non-tradition textile industry is fast developing and will soon become a sunrise industry.

Chapter 20

Modern Management Methods in Textile Industry

In recent years many state-of-the-art management techniques have emerged on the scene. Most talked about amongst them are Total Quality Management (TQM), Total Preventive Maintenance (TPM), Computer Integrated Management (CIM), Supply Chain Management (SCM), Enterprise Resource Planning (ERP), and Product Data Management (PDM). Sooner or later, new systems will confuse as to what these approaches intend or which to adopt.

Earlier also many progressive textile enterprises endorsed Management by Objectives (MBO), applied R&D techniques, and introduced Quality Circles. Regrettably, due to lack of commitment or faulty implementations in many cases they failed to muster the potential benefits from these systems. But one must realise that with emerging global challenges and dramatically changed marketplace it has become harder for a company to achieve its objective of making profits. Further in order to maintain a competitive advantage a company now need to come out of the shackles of traditional framework and adopt some novel and effective management system to operate. Simultaneously the manufacturing facilities have to undergo a major transition.

Non-Sustainable Growth

In the years bygone all around performance in the textile mills was good and hefty bottom-lines made one believe that everything is well within the industry. There was hardly any other measuring tool in hand to judge the health of a business enterprise for its sustainable growth. Further, regulated industrial growth and closed economy provided little scope for market competitiveness, therefore the quality and the price of the product offered by the mills was final. In such a scenario, only those few enterprises with a mission and a vision for the future, who spiritedly nurtured progressive management techniques could sustain development.

Now that functioning have become harder due to global competition, industry is so pre-occupied in its survival game that it can hardly indulge in the 'luxuries' of prevalent management concepts. Under the circumstances it was heartening to note that some textile companies could make noticeable success through TQM techniques. Some of these companies could increase its efficiency-level and decrease the cost of manufacturing considerably.

Total Quality Management

Total Quality Management, or TQM, is an American perception of managing quality. It is derived from Total Quality Control (TQC) system, which originated from Japan. The main difference is that TQM focuses largely on management and management technique whereas TQC lay emphasis on integrated development of product and processes. Looking through the history of development of these systems one can find that Japan developed this system to implement *Kaizen,* a Japanese word that means improvement. Moreover it means continuing improvement in personal life, home life, social life, and working life. When applied to the workplace *Kaizen* means continuing improvement involving everyone, managers and workers alike.

Japanese Industrial Standard, JIS Z 8101-1981, defines quality control (QC) as a system of techniques for economically producing goods and services that meet the customers' requirement. *Kaizen* provides the philosophy and driving force for designing quality. Thus TQC is a technique in the hands of management, which provide a platform for bringing continuing improvement in quality to satisfy customers and that too with economical operations. Similarly TQM is also customer focused and apply customer-surveying tool like quality functional deployment (QFD) to translate customers requirement of quality into technical, process and organisational requirements.

TQM also provides management with a tool to measure activities and processes within a company, against goals for improvement. Thus management become more informed to take factual decisions. In nutshell, Total Quality Management can provide organisations with the impetus for positive change, stimulating the workforce and creating an environment that gives a company the competitive edge for designing for quality. Because quality drives both revenue and cost, it is a potent driver for competitive advantage.

Corporate Mission and Vision

Some of the tools used in TQM techniques are value-added analysis, process flow mapping, and design of experiments through *Taguchi* methods to improve the implementation of total quality control in Japan. The activities of QC department of most of the textile mills in India are limited to performing physical tests on the quality parameters of the intermediate and finished products in the value added chain. Statistical Quality Control (SQC) methods are also used to evaluate the significant limits in which the quality of the product fall.

Raw material control is the first step of quality management required for a modern spinning mill to survive in today's competitive market. Some mills carry out technical evaluation of raw materials in relation to desired quality of yarns, fabrics and finished products with test trial runs in real time before purchasing bulk materials.

However, it is essential to analyse data timely and correctly since, say, unsuitable cotton types, worn out card wires, and incorrect machine settings can threaten fabric quality and in turn bottom-line. Similarly serious efforts are required to establish the effect of change of process parameters, say, roller settings and draft ratios, application of newer dyeing recipe, finishing agent, or change in the stitch length in knitting and garment assembly line on quality, productivity and manufacturing cost. A wrong labelling, packaging or invoicing and untimely despatches can cause havoc at customer's end. Therefore, a company needs tools and techniques that identify problem areas, and simplify and improve the processes on continuous basis, that are extremely critical to quality and customer satisfaction programme. Companies operating within the framework of TQM derive competitive advantage over others. Actually TQM programme defines corporate mission and vision.

Leading Edge Technology

Thanks to the state-of-the-art computerised testing equipment, now it is possible to analyse data over an established period of time that provides a valuable tool for future decision making in the optimisation of process machinery. Similarly with established benchmarks for quality levels and machinery performance, predicting future performance and production levels is possible. With the advanced optical sensor technology, it is possible now to reduce or eliminate neps, long thin places, barré, and short fiber content that affect product quality and ultimately profits.

With the state of art equipment fabric faults are now inspected objectively. Previously there was always a certain amount of subjectivity in the inspection of fabric, what one person consider a flaw might be different to what somebody else considers a defect. Further these faults are marked and classified according to standards and the system ensures that all faults are found and the source can be traced. Now technology is available to simulate fabrics based on tested fibre and yarn characteristics without weaving an inch of fabric. For driving a competitive advantage it will be essential for progressive companies to use leading edge technology within the framework of TQM.

Human Resource Management

TQM is a costly investment, therefore before implementing TQM programme it is essential to understand the needs of the company. It should also be understood that the amount of training that is involved before any visible results are realised is tremendous. There can be internal resistance to change, which could be a barrier in the implementation of the programme. To make TQM a success it requires both behavioural and cultural change in all the functional areas of a company. Since high quality performance of an organisation is the result of profitability and productivity through people, it is therefore essential to integrate Human Resource Management (HRM) with TQM. Taking clue from companies that failed in TQM one could easily find that those companies underplayed the individual factors or other problems of the working staff.

It is interesting to note that early developers of Total Quality Management systems fully realised that individuals were key to successful attainment of quality goals. Customers were identified not only external to the system, but also internally. Therefore gurus of TQM emphasised on the point that supervisors and managers operating the system need core skills. They need to have basic understandings about management, processes, and leadership to adequately operate within a Total Quality Management System. This leads to another aspects of TQM that is training and development, empowerment of the people, and preparing them for absorbing quality as a way of life. Obviously to operate such a system it would require strong and skilful leadership and committed workforce. In this period of globalisation how long textile companies will avoid adopting modern management methods?

Chapter 21
Computer Aided Management in Textile Industry

The textile industry operates under different production environments than do most other process industries. For example textile has specialised and diversified manufacturing process and control technologies with a complex value chain from raw materials to finished products to consumer. The wool processing cycle is completely different from the cotton cycle, which in its turn has little in common with silk production. Denim requires altogether different processing route and machinery than knitted fabrics. The diversity in processing types e.g. spinning, weaving, dyeing, finishing, garment manufacturing and packaging even causes variations in production management.

With these diversities in hand globalisation is becoming a big challenge to textile industry, because countries that are able to produce higher-quality goods at lower prices and cope up with increasingly shorter delivery times have competitive edge. Sooner or later textile enterprises in India require restructuring its production methods and the way they conduct business. For instance enterprises require analysing market responses and act, effectively and quickly because it is tough and competitive world where other producers are always snapping at others heals. Some big players in textiles have realised that information technology holds tremendous promise for addressing all of these issues in this period of globalisation.

Computer Integrated Manufacturing

The basic principle of effective functioning in a manufacturing and marketing enterprise is making sure that everyone in the organization has access to the right data at the right time and in the right form to allow it to be analysed and acted upon quickly. Making information systems, internal and external to an organisation, strong has now become a key factor in the success of a company. Textile manufacturing with its diversity of systems involved in shop-floor management, maintenance and quality control needs an appropriate information system that is capable of comprehending and managing all its production needs in an integrated manner.

Elsewhere in the world Computer Integrated Manufacturing (CIM) is fast becoming the de facto choice for linking manufacturing applications. CIM harmonise all manufacturing operations into a single manageable system that provides vital information regarding productivity and quality. This system also gives the feedback as to how each change in the manufacturing process affects the entire production system. It obviously involves some level of automation, computers, networking and communication technologies in the co-ordination of a company. By now all technologies that are needed to integrate a textile company has been developed.

Computer Control Processes

The textile industry have been driven forward by continual advances in automation process. The man-made fibre industry was one of the first textile industries to use computers to control its processes. Computerised monitoring in the fibre-forming process collects data from various important machine and process parameters and transmit the same to machine controllers. The computer can control such things as temperature, pressure, speed and flow rate in the extrusion process. Similarly spinning process technology from raw material retrieval to palletising, conditioning and packing of the finished product can be almost completely controlled by computers.

Auto-vision and sliver watch systems can remove the contamination of cotton in the opening lines and at sliver forming stages. Automatic feeding or transport systems are available between any two sets of machines. Autolevelling devices can ensure sliver evenness. Automatic doffing of full bobbins and removals of the empty bobbins are available. In ring spinning, control of spindle speed, monitoring of yarn breaks and auto-piecing devices are installed. Electronic yarn clearer installed on auto-winding machines can remove objectionable faults.

In weaving line computerised monitoring and recording of warp data, size formulation, size-box settings, and affected warp length are all possible. The use of microprocessors in weaving has resulted in the control of value settings, warp tension, start procedure, pick finding and filling patterns. The computer systems give users a wide range of information such as machine utilisation, efficiency, runtime and downtime analysis, produced picks, end of warp prediction, shift, daily, weekly and monthly reports.

Computer control devices in dyeing have been around since the late sixties. Alternate dye recipes with costs are available to match the customer given colours on any substrate. In dyeing machines control systems have been deployed for data collection, and supervision of timed sequences during the process cycle. Control systems can also be used to measure flow-rates, volumetric filling and rinsing, pH values, and temperature gradients. Fabric inspection systems are now fully computerised and are available to monitor defects on run time of looms. Shade variations across the width of the fabric can be detected in the same way as human eyes would detect it.

Real Time Monitoring

Real time monitoring and production reporting is one of the primary functions of a CIM system for a textile plant. Through a Graphical User Interface (GUI), users are constantly informed about the production and quality details of yarns, fabrics' sorts, colours processed and garments finished and packed. Tracking technologies, such as bar coding, allow the amount and whereabouts of work-in-process to be monitored. Powerful analysis tools allow quick identification of poor performing machines and bottlenecks in planning, resulting in an optimal usage of production capacities. With today's small order quantities and short delivery times, scheduling has become a critical function for the textile mill.

Overseas buyers are usually interested to know the status of their order supply, or give instructions regarding change in the style, colours or weave. Many a times they increase or decrease the order quantities. Accordingly spin plan can be altered, loom allocation can be readjusted and sequence of colour application in dyeing can be remade. To cope up requirements of the customers, computerised systems offer the planning department an interactive tool allowing them to optimise machine loading based on real time information. With all time access to this actual information on the shop floor one can react faster to customer's queries and solve problems before they occur. Using the World Wide Web, the salesman can give immediate and correct information about deliveries. Many textile companies operate on multiple production sites with centralised head office. They can use WWW module to centralise production management reports from all sites through the company's Intranet infrastructure and can even share information with their customers.

Supply Chain Management

Many textile companies already use computer systems, mostly

customised software modules for individual departments such as accounting, human resource and material management. Now dedicated integrated business systems are available for textile companies, better known as Enterprise Resource Planning (ERP), which can help organisation run all business processes such as processing sales orders, production planning, maintenance and quality control, materials management, accounting, sales and distribution. All these functions are interconnected seamlessly through a network of computers and any action in one department will automatic update its effect on other departments.

Lately world over there is an extremely high proportion of manufacturing to customer order. The fashion industry imposes short seasons and forecast instability. On top of it the textile processes have more variables and quality grades as well as many different units of measure. Production is subject to batch, lot, and serial number identification. Such specialised operations as the dye house have unique characteristics. These diversities sometimes lead to high inventories of raw materials, work-in-process and finished goods, which overburden the textile companies. The solution to these problems lies in Supply Chain Management system that can be nested into ERP. This system electronically links all participants in the supply chain of a textile plant from raw materials, consumables and spares suppliers, yarns to fabrics to finished products and to customers. Many apparel manufacturers in foreign countries have reduced their portion of the supply cycle through electronic links with retailers that allow them to see what is selling and anticipate re-orders.

The first logical step in the sequence of adopting hi-tech information technologies is a required degree of automation of production processes. New textile projects can plan it better with the state-of-the-art machinery. This may follow with CIM and individual modules of ERP. Manufacturing and exporting companies may like to take to total integration along with supply chain package. Sooner or later big textile players will need to adopt some degree of information technologies to meet the emerging challenges of the new millennium.

Chapter 22

Revamping Textile Education

Change is imminent and the duration of each successive technological change that would occur is narrowing down. For example, in the sixties one could not imagine that manual knotting operations in the cone winding would be replaced by automatic knotting and soon thereafter, with splicing. On-line monitoring of yarn faults always remained a distant dream for the textile technologists, which became a reality on the dawn of the day. Pick insertions with the help of shuttles was thought to be the final in the weaving technology till weft yarns found its way in the warp shed with the help of projectiles, air and even water in quick successions. Till late seventies, mechanical jacquards were considered to be a revolutionary innovation of the century till CAD/CAM not only replaced fabric designing but also held promise for more revolutionary changes in the technology in the current millennium.

Globalisation of Textile Education

With the advent of computerisation the administrative, financial and marketing operations of the companies are witnessing revolutionary changes and the textile industry dealing with the most important necessity of human beings is already under stress for change. Till recently, Enterprise Resource Planning (ERP), supply change management, and marketing on the Internet were not even dreamt in India, but these system approaches leapfrogged to a sudden reality. In order to be successful in the today's highly competitive global marketplace, it is imperative that all companies operating in the field of textiles possess a reservoir of highly skilled and proficient manpower. These technologists and executives should be well equipped to cope up with the rapid changes that are taking place in the manufacturing and the information technology vis-à-vis the global economy.

Elsewhere in the world, they have realised this situation and are gearing themselves accordingly. For instance, Philadelphia College of

Textiles and Science (USA), Shenkar College of Textile Technology and Fashion (Israel), and Reutlingen School of Textiles and Business (Germany), have developed a Master of Science program in "Global Textile Marketing" which will provide a truly global educational experience for industry executives. The program provides graduates with a unique educational background that will prepare them to play important leadership roles in the world's largest manufacturing industry. There are also some recent developments in Europe with a view to establishing close educational co-operation with the United States of America and Japan.

Textile Courses

At present most of the textile institutions of India offer two courses in textiles, namely, technology and science. The graduate courses in textile engineering and technology deals with design, research, develop and implement systems for 'fiber to fabric' production, handling and utilisation. The two specialised disciplines of textile technology include spinning and weaving. The fresh graduates in the textile technology are positioned in the industry for manufacturing supervision, in-plant and design engineering, product and process development, research, quality control and technical services. Their abilities are supposed to combine many of the talents, backgrounds and characteristics of mechanical, chemical, civil, electrical, industrial, and materials engineering. Lately the textile technologists have also found their way in the corporate management and responsible positions that lead to key, decision-making levels early in their careers.

The other courses are textile science and textile chemistry. Textile science mostly deals with textile raw materials, their properties, textile physics and testing, product characteristics, designs, structures, and applications in the consumer and industrial items beside managerial techniques, quality control and product marketing/merchandising. Textile chemistry in addition deals with textile processing and these graduates find jobs in dyeing and finishing mills, and dyes manufacturing and marketing organisations. The graduates with textile science find jobs in fibre, carpets, furnishings, fabric and apparel manufacturing related industries as production co-ordinators, research and development officers, textile designers, marketing and after sales services.

Foundation of garment manufacturing and fashion-related courses is textile science. They do impart basic knowledge of textile science in the fashion and designing institutions. Barring few, government and privately run prestigious institutions in the metropolis, large number of other so called institutions for fashion and textile designing that have mushroomed all over, are hardly equipped even with the basic facilities, equipment and trained faculty necessary for conducting these courses. It is highly unethical to 'shop' these educational packages, in disguise of much hyped profession of fashion designing, without any valid contents in it.

Changing Trends

The educational program of reputed textile institutions of the world now focus more on the business environment along with dealing the emerging technologies. Core business skills, including finance, marketing, human resource development and newer production technologies are all covered with a particular emphasis on textiles, apparel and fashion management. These institutions of the world now offer courses to prepare students for understanding the significant intercultural management, environmental and ethical factors that can have a major impact on organisations operating in a global environment. Since automation and computers are now used widely within the fields of textile design and clothing manufacture, learning about their application is an important part of textile study. These institutes are equipped with advanced computer aided design and manufacturing facilities in the weave, knit and print studios and workshops.

Department of textiles at University of Manchester Institute of Science and Technology (UMIST) offer undergraduate and diploma level modular courses in Textile Technology and Management, Clothing Engineering and Management, Management and Marketing of Textiles, beside the routine courses of Textile Science and Technology. Textile University of China offers separate under graduate and post graduate courses in Textile Processing Technology, Industrial Textiles, Textile Composites, Textile processing automation and conveyer applications, which also include information technology in textile mills. Similarly, competitive, consumer driven global markets are a core concept of the Apparel and Textiles Master of Science program of Auburn University, USA.

Change Agents

Almost every State of India has one or two diploma level textile institutions including one for North Eastern States. The important degree level textile institutions are Indian Institute of Technology, Delhi, Technological Institute of Textiles and Sciences, Bhiwani (Haryana), Government Textiles Institute, Kanpur, PSG College of Technology, Coimbatore, Victoria Jubilee Technical Institute, Bombay and recently set up SSM Institute of Textile Technology, Tamilnadu. Besides there are degree level textile colleges in W.Bengal and Baroda also. IIT-Delhi has well equipped testing laboratory and workshop. This institution is considered to be more research oriented. Post graduate research scholars turned out by it have made their mark as faculty in textile institutions abroad and many are working on research and administrative posts in Government run organisations in India.

Special mention may be made of TIT-Bhiwani. A great visionary and industrialist of India late Dr. G.D.Birla set up this institution in the year 1943 under Birla Education Trust. Beside a well-equipped laboratory and workshop, a large textile mill is attached with this institute for training the students under actual mill conditions. This is a unique feature of the institute, which has no parallel in this part of the world. The practical training imparted by the institute well prepare its graduates to face the functioning realities of textile mills of India. The institute also draws many students from foreign countries. Apart from graduate level courses in textile technology and textile chemistry, of late this institute also started a postgraduate level course in textile management science.

To meet the challenges that face us in this millennium it is important that our institutions imparting textile-related courses play an important part. Most of the textile institutions of India have yet to catch up with the rapidly changing global scenario. The faculty of some of these institutions may require extensive retraining and major reorientation of the course contents, besides improvisation in the pedagogy. The technological changes that are taking place along with mass customisation approach have necessitated these changes in the educational programmes for future technologists on whose shoulders the industry would rest. These changes have inevitably caused some sort of conflict between academia and industry, with both positive and negative results. In the ultimate scenario, textile institutions will have to assume greater responsibility to train and prepare manpower, which are in tune with the present day's industry needs in global prospective, and who may play the role of effective change agents.

Chapter 23

Textile Architecture and Interior Décor

Architecture in its crude form was practised even by our ascendants. They made use of animal skins, mud, wood and stones to build sort of dwelling units to protect them from vagaries of weather. Thereafter began the era of bricks, mortar, glass, steel and now aluminium to build modern buildings. In the modern era, without our much cognisance, temporary textile structures, such as tents and canopies, have formed a part in our everyday life. Underneath these structures we celebrate all types of events, social, cultural, religious or political. Likewise the interior of our houses are decorated with textiles in the form of curtains, upholstery, floor coverings, tapestry, and beautiful paintings done on canvass fabrics.

Traditionally fabric has always been associated with tents, coverings and temporary shelters, but rarely with permanent structures. Lately a new concept of using textile materials in the field of construction engineering and architecture is emerging worldwide. Permanent structures are being built for various functional areas. This has opened new vistas for the textile industry. With immense possibilities to exploit textile structures, designs and colours it has also created a new space for the Architects. Moreover this new trend combines aesthetics with functionality, preserve valuable resources, have short construction times, and possess high durability and low costs.

Textile Buildings

Large structures and buildings are being constructed using textile membranes, which are considered to be the most modern and innovative construction materials. The textile materials used are coated with flame retardant so these buildings are less prone to fire-hazards. The buildings include industrial undertakings, sports stadiums, and trade fare and transport facilities. Beside these buildings, there are over bridge coverings, shopping malls and pizzas, housings and thousand of other employment that the flexibility of the textile structures allows.

There are innumerable examples of these buildings, which has come around the world. Some of these buildings are a Sports Stadium at Stuttgart, Massy Station in France, Airport Hanger at Munich, Columbus Centre of Baltimore, USA and Automobile Exhibition Pavilion of BMW, Germany. Latest additions are a Malaysian Railway Station, a Chilean Shopping Centre and an American Theatre. The structural design of these buildings is said to be such that the structure weight and the external loads are supported by the pressurised air inside the enclosures, which is regulated promptly and in real time with the changes in the external load conditions.

Flexible Structures

The flexibility with which textile structures can be used and the pleasant working atmosphere they offer are said to be the decisive advantage over brick and mortars. Varieties of shapes, which can be achieved with textile membranes, were not possible with brick and steel and other traditional materials. The manufacturers of these materials claim that double-coated, insulated structures, which can be built with textile membranes, help save energy besides providing desired natural light with a right degree of translucency in a textile roof. The architectural possibilities range from light roof coverings to air-conditioned enclosures. Above all prefabricated textile structures have reduced construction times.

By using these textile membranes industrial buildings can be completed with a pre-determined time frame. Since these structures can be easily and rapidly assembled and disassembled, they offer the possibilities of easy re-location of enterprises or houses if circumstances demand so. There is another aspect of the versatile uses of textile structures. These have also been employed in the areas of environmental protection and for controlling smell and noise emission. Rubbish dumps and sewage treatment basins have been constructed since these fabrics have a high resistance to chemicals.

Innovative Materials

These modern day textile building membranes are composite materials, most of which consist of highly stable glass or polyester fibers coated with synthetic PVC or PTFE materials. The manufacturers of these materials claim that these membranes are more stable than those of steel reinforcements and girders and posses a structural life of more than 15 years. In addition these membranes are coated with a high-quality surface sealant, flame retardant, decay- resistant, and anti-fungal chemicals and are weatherproofed. Other than these, synthetic ropes made of aramide materials are now being used excessively in primary structures and are replacing heavy steel cables in many areas.

Composites of carbon fibre fabrics coated with polymers compose high load structures and hold promise in the textile architecture industry. These composites have already been used as folding beams and associated engineering for high performance bodies of sailing vessels and aircraft. Fibreglass, another manufactured mineral fibre is extensively used as insulation materials in building construction. Fibreglass cloth is especially suited for fire resistant applications. Increasingly textile fabrics are now being accepted as a sixth building material, an ideal complement to wood, bricks, cement, metal and glass. Reportedly architects and designers are of the opinion that these textile structures will grow in popularity since it is easier with them to design structures, analyse loads, and visualise exteriors. And all this can be done with the aid of computers. With so many salient features textile architecture is likely to make a major break-through in the present millennium.

Interior Decor

Interior decor is an art of planning and designing of man-made spaces, a part of environmental design and closely related to architecture. In some European countries, where this profession is well established, it is known as interior architecture. The human desire to create a pleasant environment is as old as civilisation itself. The history of textiles as an important component of interior designing ranges from early Egyptian and oriental patterns to the present. Evidence obtained from excavations near the Caspian Sea indicated that before the development of weaving, fibres were probably interlaced to produce a simple form of plaited basket-work matting even before 6000 BC.

Findings in burial mounds in southern Siberia, 2,400 years old, indicated that woven textiles, beside furs and leather, were used as floor coverings and wall hangings. Even from ancient times the styles that developed in interiors and in interior furnishings were always symbolic of the social structure of the society that created them. During Mughal periods Palaces were literally covered in textiles. The decorative and architectural use of luxurious textiles symbolically reminded royal visitors of the power and the wealth of the rulers. Carpets on the floor, pillows for seating, tapestry-hanging screens in windows and doorways with niche patterns, gold brocades, rich velvets, colours and textures enlivened the interiors. Sometimes carpets provided the actual architecture; for example, when they were used in the construction of portable tent compounds for royal visits. The layout of the Mughal palace was re-created in these tent compounds.

With the development of newer fibres, woven patterns and printed designs of the 20th century, textiles are now increasingly sought for interior designing. For indoor environment curtains, window dressings, veils, and upholstery with a complete range of colours in solids, prints and decorative with ethnic motifs are available for Interior designers to exploit. With the introduction of digital printing short runs of customised printed designs are now available. Users of these fabrics now look for fast and eco-friendly colours, minimum shrinkage on washing, stain-free and anti-fungal qualities. Many of the interior designers now work closely with textile designers. The art of interior designing no longer remains an exclusive domain of architects.

Safety Decor

Beside comfort and pleasant ambience for which textile materials are used, lately architects have started laying more importance to safety factor when designing interiors of hotels, restaurants, cinemas, theatres, and offices. Research into the causes of fire at various functional places has proved that furnishing fabrics can help fire to spread. Therefore the interior decorators are now seeking more and more those fabrics that possess flame retardant qualities.

Special synthetic fibres have been developed that are now widely used in developed countries for curtains and as upholstery fabrics, especially when the strict flammability standard for public occupancies are required to be met. These fibers are aramids, PBI, melamine, saran and sulfar, which provide a very high degree of protection. These manufactured fibers are made from heat-stable polymers that do not melt or burn. Wool furnishing and upholstery fabric, though costly, has the inherent resistance to flame and heat that make it one of the safest of all upholstery fabrics.

Building development authorities and fire protection regulations in various countries are contemplating to make flame retardant fabrics mandatory in case of textiles used for furnishing public utility buildings. Insurance companies have their own requirements in this respect. It is most likely that in this new millennium people will attach more importance to safety decor.

Chapter 24
Health Hazards of Textiles

Environment and health are the two growing concerns in the world today. With the development of modern technologies the hitherto unknown factors causing health problems are now being surfaced out. Everyday new discoveries are revealing that many food items of human consumption could cause cancer, heart problems, and other diseases. These items are either banned for production or warned against use. To address these growing concerns newer products and ecological sustainable technologies are being developed.

Textiles being the basic requirement of human cannot be isolated from these growing concerns. In this respect people connected with consumer protectionism, health medicine and researchers keep scrutinising various aspects of textile production and usage against any health hazards. The speed, with which the researches are unfolding the potential health hazards components in textile production and usage, it may become difficult for many developing countries to keep pace with the stringent requirements of modern day textiles and the associated technological and structural changes. Before these problems take a serious turn textile industry of India needs to address them on war footing.

Chemical hazards

From fibre to fabric, manufacturing processes of textiles involve usage of various chemicals in the form of pesticides, organic and inorganic compounds. Lately it has been discovered that some of these chemicals are potential health hazards. Developed countries have either banned or restricted in use many dyes and chemicals in the production of textiles. One can cite the example of ban on azo dyes and restrictions in the use of formaldehyde by some countries. According to a health report from USA there was increase in cancer rates between 1950 and 1986 by 37%. This was partly attributed to increasing use of pesticides.

Ironically, this was besides the fact that modern day pesticides are supposedly less lethal than the early days of calcium arsenate and DDT used before World War II. However the reality that the increase in cancer rates can not be attributed entirely to the use of present day pesticides, does not make these chemicals lesser poisonous. Unfortunately developing countries are the biggest consumers of pesticide, dyes and chemicals. On top of this health and environmental regulations are extremely limited in these countries. Developed countries are taking recourse to plantation of organic and bio-engineered cottons, which are grown without the use of pesticides. It is now a matter of time before these countries ban importing cotton products harvested with pesticides.

Occupational Hazards

Further there is now growing realisation that safe and contamination free atmospheric conditions need to be provided at the work place to minimise hazards to the health of workers. From past research, it is suspected that inhalation of fibre in the lung may result in scarring of the lung or lung cancer. Recently National Occupational Health & Safety Commission of Australia made some epidemiological studies on human exposures to synthetic mineral fibres such as glass fibre, mineral wool and ceramic fibres. The studies revealed that the ill effects on health depend on the amount of fibre inhaled, the particle size, the durability in the lung and the chemical and biological reactivity of the fibre.

The chances of the diseases are more if the inhaled fibre resides in the lungs for longer duration. Very fine fibres, less than 0.2 um diameter, have more chances to remain in the lungs and are the most hazardous. However in most cases deposited fibres are transported out from the lung by scavenger cells or via natural clearance mechanisms provided in the human system. Notwithstanding these findings, it is most likely that in the near future it become imperative for the textile mills to provide suitable and dust free working atmosphere in the worker's breathing zone through appropriate engineering controls, revised work practices and, where necessary, by the introduction of personal protective equipment.

Azo Dyes; Myth and Reality

Germans and Dutch are most environmentally aware people. Due to health reasons Germany banned the use of azo dyes on any product, which frequently come into direct contact with human body. The Dutch law, on the other hand, covers only clothing, footwear and bed linen.

Any infringement of these regulations is treated as a criminal offence in these countries. Prior to this ban there was enormous media campaign involving the accusation that textiles are health hazard and textile auxiliaries and colourants are supposed to cause skin problems. Scientist are of the view that if these dyes enter the human body, say by absorption through skin, reductive action may occur within the body as a result of normal metabolic process. Azo colours, under reduction conditions, might liberate aromatic amines, which can cause cancer in the human being and heritable variations in the progeny.

According to a medical research, bladder cancer is found in increasing frequency in certain individuals working in commercial dye and PCB plastic industry, beside amongst heavy smokers. Smoking has always been the major risk factor for cancer in its various deadly forms. Surprisingly, many people in developed countries continue to smoke unmindful of connected health hazards, whereas they support banning the azo dyes. Out of about 3,000 commercial dyes used all over the world about 65% of the colours used in textile dyeing and printings are based on azo chemistry. However out of 20 types of amines in azo group shown in the banned list only five have been proved to be the cause for cancer, others are still suspects.

Ever since Congo red, the first azo dye of any significance that was synthesised in 1884 from Benzedrine, azo compounds have remained the most important class of dyes up to the present day. Azo dyes are easy to produce and their cost of production is low. Moreover these dyes posses high colour strength and brilliance. But due to ban imposed by Germany and Netherlands, dye manufacturers are constantly replacing such types of dyestuffs. Likewise Europe, Japan and the US had placed limits on the amount of formaldehyde in textiles, which has irritant effect on mucous membranes and the skin.

Many believe that such types of bans are only to protect the textile industries of developed countries. Others believe that the noise over azo dyes is more of a myth. This class of people believes that since some of the European countries have developed a substitute for azo dyes, they want to force other countries to buy their products. Whatever the reasons may be one thing is unfortunate that these restrictions have made textile production difficult with associated economic strains in the developing countries. To cope with this changed environment the dye manufacturers are now undergoing expensive restructuring.

Carpeting

Americans are very health conscious people. Lately exposure to indoor air contaminants, believed to be caused by wall to wall carpeting, has become an area of health concern. It is found that on an average a person spends 80% to 90% of his or her time indoors, at home and at work. Therefore quality of the indoor air is an important aspect from health point of view. In this respect carpets are found to be health hazard since they are considered haven for dust mites, the microorganism that are commonly found in homes. According to a finding of Banglore Allergy Centre, dust mites are more responsible for several types of allergies than pollution.

Dust mites could cause bronchial asthma and allergies leading to sneezing, running nose and nasal blockage. Therefore ventilation system in a building with wall to wall carpet is an important aspect in maintaining quality of indoor air to avoid health problems. In order to meet these problems a French company Rhovyl has developed a technology to produce fibres, which are repellent to dust mites. The long lasting fibre kills the mites and prevents further infestation. The company claims that by using products made of these fibres the frequency with which patient has to change bed linen, pillows, blankets and vacuum carpets and mattresses will be reduced.

Medicated Textiles

A recent study conducted by the University of Arizona showed that between 10 and 20 percent of fabrics coming out of a washing machine were contaminated. This is because connected pipes and crevices of the machine become residence for E. coli, salmonella or hepatitis A, potentially deadly bacteria. To combat bacterial contamination, which may rest in the fibers and fabrics of everyday clothing, some biotechnology companies are coming up with fibres and fabrics with Antimicrobial agent. These agents are embodied into the fiber during its manufacturing process, which assures the longevity of antibacterial in the clothing even after much washing.

Some companies have claimed that the Antimicrobial agent could be blended into the manufacturing process of all kind of fabrics, including cotton, wool, polyester, nylon and acrylic. With this unique technology and application process, everything from hotel bed sheets and pillow covers, mattresses and carpeting to bandages will be safe from potentially harmful bacteria. These fibres are also finding usage in the manufacturing of socks, underwear, gloves, hats, scarves, and sleeping Bags. More and more of these type of newer technologies and medicated textiles will emerge on the scene in this millennium.

Chapter 25

Towards Pollution Free Production

An industry is like a living organism. It breathes in gases, and exhales other gases. It consumes materials, and uses energy to change their form into products and waste materials outputs. The energy flow through an industrial firm looks like the energy flow through a green plant, our planet's oldest industrial firms. Nature maintained a remarkable balance in the ecosystem until man-induced industrial metabolism meddled with it. Traditionally, the textile industry is very intense consumer of energy, water, and chemicals. Dyeing and finishing operations uses about 60% of the total energy consumed in the textile industry. Environmental problems associated with the textile industry are that associated with water and air pollution. Some of the chemicals discharged are toxic. Other environmental issues now considered equally important and relevant to the textile industry include air emissions, notably Volatile Organic Compounds.

Atmospheric pollution is now a major problem facing all the countries of the world. For a long time, developed countries were the home for energy and pollution-intensive industries. Now these industries are growing twice as fast in developing countries. This responsibility shift to developing countries brings in the pressures for a pollution free production system. Pollution prevention is a responsibility as sacrosanct to the textile industry as to others.

To conform to the environmental management directive, it may be that EU will trade or do business with those companies that demonstrate adherence to the standards for pollution free production. There are previous examples of such restrictions in case of child labour in carpet industry and that on azo dyes. Textile industry should take the environmental issues seriously and gear up to meet the impending challenges.

Textile Pollutants

The problem of wastewater from textile industry is rather complicated, since this industry uses a great variety of raw materials, intermediate products, and chemicals. Methods of production also vary widely. The quantity of wastewater discharged into sewerage per production unit is roughly 90 to 100 per cent of total water consumption for the processing. The qualitative characteristics of wastewater are variable largely and, even in the same industry branch, depend on the use of dyestuffs and raw materials types, liquor to material ratios, and the type of machines they employ. The two main sources of pollution in the textile process are the natural impurities extracted from the type of fibre under processing along with the chemicals used. Other factors, which determine effluent quantity and quality, include the number of operations used and the degree to which they preserve water and chemicals in a particular manufacturing plant.

Wool scouring effluents have high BOD compared to cotton finishing effluents that contain no grease and have a relatively low solids content. Synthetic finishing effluents are generally lower in volume than those generated in cotton finishing, but may contain toxic substances, especially from those dyeing streams where chemical dyes with a metallic ion content are used more widely. Also of particular concern are some specific compounds that are toxic to aquatic life. According to a technical report of UNIDO the sources of major metal pollutants, i.e., zinc, copper, chromium, etc. are likely to be the dyes used in wet processing operations.

The causes of air pollution attributed to textile industry are mainly from emissions from textile processing, excluding boiler emissions. Oil mist and organic emissions are produced when textile materials containing knitting and lubricating oils, platicisers, and other materials that can volatilise or be thermally degraded into volatile substances, are subjected to heat. Processes that can be sources of oil mist include stentering, calendaring, heat setting, drying, and curing. Carbonisation of wool and some types of spray dyeing produce acid mist. Solvent processing operations such as dry cleaning and scouring releases vapours. The other cause is dust and lint produced during the spinning of natural fibres and synthetic staple as well as by carpet shearing. Add to above be the releases of excessive nitrogen from the production and use of nitrogen fertilizers to the burning of fossil fuels in automobiles, power generation plants, and industries. This has doubled the natural annual rate at which fixed nitrogen enters the land-based nitrogen cycle, and the pace is likely to accelerate.

Environmental Impacts

Due to water and air pollution, serious environmental consequences are already becoming apparent. Scientists have discovered that the net effect of both air and water pollutants have already weaken the biosphere. Industrial pollutants along with other human activities have contributed to the same. There has been increased concentration of greenhouse gases, that is nitrous oxide, leading to greenhouse effect, i.e., the warming of the atmosphere of the earth. Nitrous oxide is a very effective heat-trapping gas in the atmosphere because it absorbs outgoing radiant heat from the Earth in infrared wavelengths that other major greenhouse gases, water vapour and carbon dioxide do not capture. By absorbing and rediating this heat back toward the Earth, nitrous oxide contributes a few percent to overall greenhouse warming.

The suspicion is that global warming will disrupt weather and climate patterns. It could lead to drought in some areas and flooding in others. Scientists are further of the view that with the concentrations of the nitrous oxide in the atmosphere, acid rains are increasing. Acid Rains accelerates the decay of building materials and paints, including irreplaceable buildings, statues, and sculptures that are part of our nation's cultural heritage. Soils in many regions are being acidified and stripped of nutrients essential for continued fertility have accelerated losses of plant and animal diversity in both aquatic and land-based ecosystems.

Synergistic to above, the untreated sewage and industrial effluents have increased BOD discharges into the water streams thereby reducing the dissolved oxygen levels in some stretches of the river, canals, or lakes endangering aquatic life. Scientist are of the opinion that leaching, that is trickling down of contaminants, may occur in farming areas, feedlots or landfills resulting in hazardous substances entering surface water, groundwater or soil. With the contamination of ground water, pollution has also raised human health concerns. Further, scientist have discovered that there have been depletion of stratospheric ozone layer that shield the earth from harmful health effects of ultraviolet radiation on humans and the environment. It also reduces the visibility. It is therefore paramount that national and international policies address to the environmental issues to slow the pace of this global change, and moderate its impacts.

Environment Management System

Both environmental law and regulated industry are experiencing dramatic changes. That revolution is about the ascendancy of Environmental Management Systems such as ISO 14000 as clear alternatives to existing environmental regulatory structures. Environmental Management is a tool for an organization to keep aware of the interactions that its products and activities have with the environment and to continuously improve the desired level of environmental performance. ISO 14000 is a series of environmental standards developed by International Standards Organization. These standards include environmental auditing, environmental performance, life cycle analysis, and environmental labelling and environmental aspects in product standards. An effective Environmental Management System is the consistent and systematic control of procedures or operations, products or services, which can have a significant impact on the environment.

A central element of the ISO 14001 standard is the "Environmental Policy" defined and carried out by the top management of the organization. This involves planning, implementation and operations, checking and corrective action, and management review. Implementation of an Environmental Management System is a rapidly growing force affecting a tremendous number of businesses worldwide. According to the data available with ISO, there were 5700 companies in the world accredited to ISO 14000 as on September 1998. There are 60 in India as compared with 49 in China. Japan tops the list with 1237 companies. U.K. and Germany have 650 ISO 14000 accredited companies and USA is with 200. Organisations should integrate the Environmental Management System with other activities. An organisation that has effectively integrated an Environmental Management System with its other business management systems is well on its way towards managing its processes to accrue the accompanying benefits.

Chapter 26

Towards Cleaner Production Paradigm

Until now, the approach to pollution control has been through either dilution or treatment. India, as many other developing countries, is still at the dilution or treatment stage. The dilution approach that involves the discharge of pollutants directly into the environment mainly relies on the assimilative capacity of the water, air, and soil to dilute or neutralise the impacts. Obviously, this approach can work if the amount of waste is small as compared to the volume of the receiving environment. Talking of textiles, in areas where there is a heavy concentration of dyeing and finishing industry, this method may not be effective.

Second, the treatment stage is to collect pollutants at the end of the process and to separate or neutralise them in various ways, usually in specially built treatment plants. Treatment often merely separates the pollutants from the waste stream, but these still have to be disposed of somewhere. Moreover, the costs of the end-of-pipe treatment approach are one of the discouraging factors for SSI to invest on this non-productive process. Reportedly, United States spent US$ 100 billion and the countries of the European Community spent more than US$ 30 billion on pollution control in 1992. However, there was little direct financial return to the industries, which incurred this expenditure. Certainly, dilution and treatment, and even recycling, are not long run solutions. Nevertheless, industries have to find a solution since the pollution can impair human health, reduce the productivity of fisheries and agriculture and damage man-made materials.

Cleaner Production

The composition of the pollution is becoming more complex. Thousands of new dyes and chemicals are introduced into the market each year to add to those already there. Moreover, stringent environmental regulations are putting pressure on industry to increase its environmental performance. It is often difficult, however, to modify existing plants at a reasonable cost. Cleaner Production, the preventive way, an evolving concept is considered a better approach to avoiding and minimising environmental problems. Increasingly both businesses and regulators are realising that Pollution Prevention is a more powerful and economical strategy. Since processes, those cause pollution also wastes raw materials. Managers are finding that they can save money by preventing pollution in the first place, while increasing efficiency.

Cleaner Production, as defined by United Nations Environment Programme, UNEP, is the continuous application of an integrated preventive environmental strategy to processes and products to reduce risks to humans and the environment. Studies reveal that the application of Cleaner Production concept is good for the environment because it reduces pollution from industry. For production processes, the application includes conserving not only the raw materials but energy also. Further, it ensures eliminating toxic processing materials and reducing the quantity and toxicity of all emissions and wastes before they leave a production process.

Cleaner Production requires application of technical expertise, improving technology, and changing management attitudes. In nutshell, the implementation of Cleaner Production technologies involves changes in human thinking and attitudes about production and the environment. Experience with Cleaner Production gained by many countries shows that the companies could make many improvements in the production processes at no or very little cost and discharge the pollutants in a cost-effective way. In India, The National Cleaner Production Centre of India, New Delhi, disseminates the Cleaner Production programmes. They have undertaken some programmes with fabric dyeing and finishing mills in Ludhiana and reports indicate encouraging results. Their activities need more exposure to the textile industry. Many Cleaner Production techniques yield substantial savings in production costs.

Alternative Technologies

According to a UNEP technical report, it is possible to lower the pollution problems in a wet processing unit by reducing the chemical loads, employing eco-friendly chemical substitutions, using alternative technologies, and processing methods. In a study it was found that very often a large margin of safety is employed while using the chemicals and many textile mills use excessive and even unnecessary chemicals. Often they add chemicals in a dye recipe to counteract a negative side effect of another ingredient instead of finding a substitute for the offending chemical. For example, a company some years ago would select a certain mineral oil or a paraffin wax on technical merit alone without any environmental considerations. It is likely, that now there is an alternative higher boiling point oil product available in the market. Further, the traditional carding oils have 100 per cent BOD values and may be replaced with non-ionic emulsifiers that have only 20 per cent BOD.

Now many processors substitute formic acid for acetic acid in dye baths. Acetic acid has a five times more BOD as compared with Formic acid. They also use single-class dyestuffs like Indigosol, pigments, etc. for dyeing blended varieties in pale shades in place of two stages dyeing using two different classes of dyes. This substitution reduces water and energy consumption with resultant reduction in wastewater and air emissions. Experts now recommend use of reverse dyeing techniques for dyeing blends of polyester-cotton fabrics. In the reverse dyeing process, the cotton with reactive is dyed first followed by dyeing of polyester component with disperse dyeing. In this way the slightly acidic disperse dye-bath serves as an after wash for the fiber reactive. This would conserve both water and energy. The UNEP report indicate that a new classes of fibre reactive dyes, e.g. triazine based will reduce the use of azo dyes and contribute to the discharge of lower concentrations of dyes during washing and rinsing.

Excess chemical usage may also result from the scoop method of chemical addition rather than precise measurement techniques. By providing specific instructions and metering equipment, one can reduce both chemical and water consumption. Experts recommend the reuse of dye-bath wherever possible. The easiest systems to manage for dye-bath reuse are dye classes that give high affinity, that is exhaustion, and which undergo minimum changes during the dyeing processes. The used dye-bath will usually be hot, over 60 degree centigrade. Thus starting the next dyeing at the highest possible temperature saves a considerable time, fresh water, chemical consumption and energy. Experiments have shown that this methodology can reduce BOD and COD loading up to 33%.

Similarly there may be various other processes and methods which may result reduction in water, chemical usage and level of energy consumption. Thus, a mill should make a careful study of the various textile processes, with respect to the minimum requirements of different chemical recipes. Experts are of the opinion that one can reduce the amount of process chemicals by 20-50% and the effluent load in terms of BOD by about 30-50% with the obvious associated benefit of lower effluent disposal and operating costs.

Green Awards

Little forethought and planning can show that business and the environment can, not only coexist but also flourish. One can emulate the example of Amoco Chemical, USA, producer of more than 1.5 billion pounds of PTA per year. PTA is the basic material for producing polyester. The company sponsored ecological studies to know the impact of their plant on the wetland and forested tracks, even before they laid the foundation of their plant. They replanted native species, provided year-round feeding plots for the wildlife. They now regularly monitor the impact of their plant on the safety of employees and the environment. Recently, Amoco Chemical developed the first full-scale anaerobic process, in which biodegradation can occur without oxygen. In a program developed by Amoco Foam Products, they've been putting their foam cafeteria trays in specially marked recycling bins. Amoco Chemical is helping to lead the way in developing new technology for recycling polystyrene foam. In 1992, their Alabama plant won President's Safety Award for a second time.

Sterling Fibers, Inc., producer of acrylic fibres, rather than just dispose of the biological treated weak wastewater stream, used the same for spray irrigation. The initial concern of the pollution control officials that this effluent might contaminate the ground water in the area was unfounded. There was no negative environmental impact from the spraying, on the other hand this proved beneficial to enhance the surrounding plant life on its property. Tests showed the 70,000 pine trees on the 80- acre site produced approximately twice the pulp of similar trees growing elsewhere in the area. Groundwater monitoring of the spray irrigation site has put all concern of contamination to the ground water to rest. The company hopes that spraying will help Sterling Fibers achieve the National Pollutant Discharge System goal of zero discharge a goal to which the company is committed to accomplish in the near future.

Glossary of words

(Other than textile words used in the articles)

A

Acid Rains

A complex chemical and atmospheric phenomenon that occurs when emissions of sulphur and nitrogen compounds and other substances are transformed by chemical processes in the atmosphere, often far from the original sources, and then deposited on earth in either a wet or dry form. The wet forms, popularly called acid rain, can fall as rain, snow or fog. The dry forms are acidic gases or particulate.

Aquatic life

Life such as fishes that grows and live underneath the surface of seawater and stretches of rivers, canals and lakes.

Archaeology

The scientific study of material remains (as fossil relics, artifacts, and monuments) of past human life and activities, in short, remains of the culture of a people.

Automation

The automatically controlled operation of an apparatus, process, or system by mechanical or electronic devices that replace human controls.

B

Benchmarking

The study of a competitor's product or business practices in order to improve the performance of one's own company. These studies may lead to benchmark standards by which quality, productivity or costs may be measured or judged.

Biochemical Oxygen Demand (BOD)

The term, biochemical oxygen demand (BOD) refers to effluent discharges. It is a measure of the amount of dissolved oxygen used by microorganisms to assimilate organic wastes. With untreated sewage and industrial effluents with high BOD discharges into the water streams, the dissolved oxygen levels in some stretches of the river, canals or lakes become so low that fish are unable to live. The greater the BOD, the greater the pollution. Oxygen is an essential ingredient to support the aquatic life. The required oxygen is readily available to the aquatic organisms in the dissolved form in the water known as dissolved oxygen. This oxygen diffuses into the aquatic system from aeration from the atmosphere and photosynthesis, and in a balanced system, it replenishes itself as rapidly as it is used. However, the decomposition of excessive amounts of organic matter such as dying algae or sewage wastes also consumes dissolved oxygen, and can limit the ability of a system to support aquatic life. That is why the State water quality standards often express minimum concentrations of dissolved oxygen which must be maintained in order to support certain levels of beneficial use. Levels of dissolved oxygen below 4-5 milligrams per litre affect fish health and levels below 2 mg/l are considered lethal to fish.

Biodegradable

Any material, which breaks down and decomposes rapidly under natural conditions and processes.

Biological treatment

A treatment technology that uses bacteria to consume waste. This treatment breaks down organic materials.

Biosphere

The portion of the earth that supports life, including the surface waters and the air. Protecting the biosphere from industry related activities are a fundamental criterion for sustainable development. The protective steps include stabilising the biosphere in the face of the threats from greenhouse gases and ozone-depleting substances, maintaining the carrying capacity of natural resource systems (forest, fisheries and agricultural land) and protecting the absorptive (assimilative) capacity of air, water, and soil from emissions and waste discharges.

Biotechnology

Techniques that use living organisms or parts of organisms to produce a variety of products, from medicines to industrial enzymes, to improve plants or animals or to develop micro-organisms for specific uses such as removing toxic from bodies of water or killing pests.

Business Process Reengineering

Restructuring and transforming a business process by a fundamental rethinking and redesign to achieve dramatic improvements in cost, quality, speed, and so on.

Buzzword

A fashionable technical word or a catchword.

C

Chemical Oxygen Demand (COD)

A measure of oxygen required for oxidising all compounds in water, both organic and inorganic.

Cleaner Production

Cleaner Production avoids industrial pollution by reducing waste generation at every stage of the production process in order to minimise or eliminate waste before any potential pollutants are created.

Cleaner Production (CP) is the continuous application of an integrated preventive environmental strategy applied to processes, products and services to increase eco-efficiency and reduce the risks to humans and the environment. For processes, CP includes conserving raw materials and energy, eliminating toxic raw materials and reducing the quantity and toxicity of all emissions and wastes. For products, CP involves reducing the negative impacts along the life cycle of a product, from raw materials extraction to its ultimate disposal.

Competitive advantage

Developing products, services, processes, or capabilities that give a company a superior business position relative to its competitors and other competitive forces.

Computer

A device that has the ability to accept data, internally store and execute a programme of instructions, perform mathematical, logical and manipulative operations on data, and report the results.

Computer Integrated Manufacturing (CIM)

An overall concept that stresses that the goals of computer use in factory automation should be to simplify, automate, and integrate production processes and other aspects of manufacturing.

Computer Monitoring

Using computer to monitor the behaviour and productivity of the workers on the job and in the workplace.

Computer-aided design (CAD)

The use of computers and advanced graphics hardware and software to provide interactive design assistance for engineering and architectural designs. Lately textile designing is also created by CAD system.

Computer-Aided Manufacturing (CAM)

The use of computer system to automate the production processes and operations of a manufacturing plant.

Cutting Edge Technology

A breakthrough technique or system approaches that alters radically the conventional way of doing things.

Cyberspace

A term used to describe vast electronic network in which everyday tasks, such as banking, research and communication, are conducted via computers.

D

Digital design

This term refers to the creation of designs, (in the present context for printing on the textile fabrics) with digital text, which is the use of numbers and digits, to express units of computer data. These designs are then directly converted to CAM system of the machines for execution.

Distributed database

The concept of distributing databases or a portion of a database at remote sites where the data is most frequently referenced. Sharing of the data is made possible through a network that interconnects the distributed databases.

Downsizing

Moving to smaller and compact work systems.

E

Eco-friendly

A product, process or a system use of which does not cause any harm to the ecology.

Ecologically Sustainable Industrial Development

Ecologically sustainable industrial development is defined as those patterns of industrialisation that enhance economic and social benefits for present and future generations without impairing basic ecological processes. The three main criteria are eco-capacity, efficiency and equity. Eco-capacity is the critical load of industrial pollutants beyond which the quality of life and the proper management of natural assets are affected.

Ecology

A branch of science concerned with the interrelationship of living things, organisms and their environments.

Economic feasibility

This aspect relates to the determination of the extent of absorption and acceptability of the output of a new unit or the additional production from an established unit in the market at the given prices.

Ecosystem

The interacting system of a biological community and its non-living environmental surroundings. If our ecosystems are impaired, we probably have not developed a long-term sustainable relationship with our environment. Although the way we determine threats to the health of ecosystems is similar to that required for human health risks. Ecological risk assessment requires examining many more organisms other than just man, thus introducing even more uncertainty. Excessive nitrogen additions can pollute ecosystems and alter both their ecological functioning and the living communities they support.

Electronic data interchange

The electronic transmission of source documents between the computers of different organisation.

Electronic funds transfer

The development of banking and payment systems that transfer funds electronically instead of using cash or paper documents such as cheques.

Electronic mail

A system for exchanging written, voice, and video voices through a network.

End-of-pipe treatment

Treating pollutants at the end of a process (by, for example, filters, catalysts and scrubbers) instead of preventing their occurrence.

Enterprise Resource Planning (ERP)

ERP is the process that integrates flow of information, which binds the entire organisation. It is a computerised system mainly used in manufacturing industries to drive competitive advantage in the production, distribution and financial areas. It is an integrated suit of application software modules providing operational, managerial and strategic information for improving productivity, quality and competitiveness.

Environmental Management Systems (EMS)

Environmental Management is a tool for an organisation to keep aware of the interactions that its products and activities have with the environment and to achieve and continuously improve the desired level of environmental performance. ISO 14000 series of standards are the model for an environmental management system.

The highest priorities are assigned to preventing pollution through source reduction and reuse, or closed loop recycling. Preventing or recycling at the source eliminates the need for off-site recycling or treatment and disposal. Elimination of pollutants at or near the source is typically less expensive than collecting, treating, and disposing of wastes. It also presents much less risk to the workers, the community, and the environment.

Epidemiology

A branch of medical science that deals with the incidence, distribution, and control of disease in a population or the sum of the factors that controls the presence or absence of a disease or pathogen.

F

Fiscal policy

Governmental policy which deal with the public revenue.

Fossil fuels

Any of a class of materials of biological origin occurring within the Earth's crust that can be used as a source of energy. Fossil fuels include coal, natural gas, petroleum, shale oil, and bitumen. They all contain carbon and were formed as a result of geologic processes from the remains of organic matter produced by photosynthesis hundreds of millions of years ago.

G

Generic name

A general and non-trademark name which relates to a class, origin or description. For example polyester is a generic name and Terelene is one of its trademarks.

Global recession

This phenomenon relates to economic slump or slowdown in the world market. Corporate are barely able to maintain profit margins. There is a loss of jobs and lay-off is on the rise, inventories are run down and outlays are cut. Demand for products and services fall sharply. Capacity utilisation of the manufacturing firms and service organisation show a downtrend. New investments are held back. Commodity and stock prices plummet.

Global warming

The consequences of the greenhouse effect, caused by rising concentrations of greenhouse gases. The suspicion is that global warming will disrupt weather and climate patterns. It could lead to drought in some areas and flooding in others. One of the most serious environmental problems that faces the world.

Globalisation

Becoming a global enterprise by expanding into global markets, using global production facilities, forming alliances with global partners, and so on.

Graphical User Interface (GUI)

A user interface such as computer monitor screen in which actions are initiated when the user selects an icon or an option from a pull down menu with mouse or a pointing device. That allows the user to interact with the software.

Greenhouse effect

The warming of the earth's atmosphere, caused by a build-up of carbon dioxide or other trace gases. Many scientists believe that this build-up allows light from the sun's ray to heat the earth but prevents a counterbalancing loss of heat.

Greenhouse gases

The gases, such as carbon dioxide, water vapour, methane, and nitrous oxides that trap the sun's heat in the lower atmosphere and prevent it from escaping into space. Major source of increased concentration in the atmosphere is the combustion of fossil fuels.

H

Hazardous waste

By-products of society that can pose a substantial hazard to human health or the environment when improperly managed.

Human Resource Management

Managing, guiding and developing a workforce producing a product or services with an aim to improve quality, productivity and profitability in an organisation.

I

Industrial recession

This phenomenon occurs when manufacturing units are barely able to maintain profit margins. There is a loss of jobs and lay-off is on the rise, inventories are run down and outlays are cut. Demand for products and services fall sharply. Capacity utilisation shows a downtrend. Investments in the new projects or extension of the existing one's are held back.

Industrial Revolution

The Industrial revolution relates to a period in eighteenth and nineteenth centuries. During this period there was drastic change and transformation from hand tools, and hand made items to machine manufactured and mass produced goods. Organised factories came up in place of cottage units. Now a machine could do a job of twenty or more people. This change generally helped life, but also with some dire consequences like workers unrest.

Information technology

A technology that uses the vast communications links to allow access to government, industry, and educational and other data banks for all users. It encompasses hardware, software, and telecommunications, data base management and other information processing technologies. Using information technology for globalisation, business process reengineering and agile competition frequently results in the development of information systems that help give a company a competitive advantage.

Internet

This is a rapidly growing network of thousands of business, educational and research networks connecting millions of computers and their users in many countries.

Intranet

A network designed to facilitate communication within an organisation, as well as with customers and partners, often refereed to as 'information highway'.

ISO 14000 standards

ISO 14000 family of standards and guidelines are primarily concerned with "environmental management". In plain language, this means what the organization does to minimise harmful effects on the environment caused by its activities.

ISO 14001 is an emerging standard entitled "Environmental Management Systems - Specification". ISO 14001 standard is the "Environmental Policy" defined by an organisation's top management. A system is then defined that ensures that the environmental policy is carried out by the organization. This involves planning, implementation and operations, checking and corrective action, and management review.

ISO 9000 standards

ISO 9000 are actually a family of standards, which are referred to under this generic title for convenience. The family consists of standards and guidelines relating to management systems, and related supporting standards on terminology and specific tools, such as auditing (the process of checking that the management system conforms to the standard).

ISO 9000 is primarily concerned with "quality management". Like "beauty", everyone may have his or her idea of what "quality" is. In plain language, the standardised definition of "quality" in ISO 9000 refers to all those features of a product (or service) which are required by the customer. "Quality management" means what the organization does to ensure that its products conform to the customer's requirements.

L

Leading Edge Technology

An innovative technology that outshine the contemporary technologies.

Life cycle Analysis

Assessment or 'cradle to grave' analysis covering the entire life of a product or a function such as extraction and processing of raw materials; manufacturing process; transport and distribution; use; reuse; maintenance; recycling; and final disposal of the product. Also covered are the use of scarce resources; releases of hazardous materials; impact on the local environment; and effects on global problems such as ozone depletion and climate change.

M

Management Information System

A management support system that produces pre-specified reports, displays, and responses on a periodic, exceptional and demand basis.

Mass customisation

This term refers to meeting individual's specification or requirement of a product in a mass production environment such as factories.

Metabolism

The chemical changes in living cells by which energy is provided for vital processes and activities and new material is assimilated, or the sum of the processes by which a particular substance is handled in the living body. Or the sum of the metabolic activities taking place in a particular environment.

Microcomputers

A very small computer, ranging in size from a 'computer on a chip' to small typewriter size unit.

Microprocessor

An integrated circuit on a single chip that makes up the central processing unit of computers, composed of silicon or other material etched with many tiny electronic circuits.

Millennium

A period of one thousand years, such as 1901 AD to 2000 AD.

Multitasking

The capability of an operating system to switch between tasks.

Mummification

A method of preserving dead bodies for a very long period. The dead bodies were cleaned, embalmed and wrapped with linen bandage and placed under a canopy. Settlers near Nile River areas, now known as Egypt, started this tradition.

N

Networking

The process of connecting computers that permits the transfer of data and programmes between users.

NPAs

Non Performing Assets. This term refers to the assets of the enterprises, created out of loan money advanced by the financial institutions and banks, which are not operating or generating enough funds to meet the liabilities of interest and instalments due to lending organisations.

O

On-line

Connected to, served by, or available through a networked computer system and under control of a central processing unit.

Optical sensor technology

Technology, which uses a device that optically scans, characters and images and generates their digital representation. It enables a computer to translate the scanned data to be used in other system.

Outsourcing

The use of outside expertise to accomplish a task, such as hiring a factory for job-work say for garment manufacturing.

Ozone depletion

Destruction of the stratospheric ozone layer, which shields the earth from ultraviolet radiation harmful to life. Certain chlorine and or bromine containing compounds that break down when they reach the stratosphere and catalyse the destruction of ozone molecules causing destruction of ozone.

Ozone layers

Found in two layers of the atmosphere, the stratosphere and the troposphere. In the stratosphere (the atmospheric layer beginning 7-10 miles above the earth's surface), ozone is a form of oxygen found naturally which provides a protective layer, shielding the earth from ultraviolet radiation's harmful health effects on humans and the environment. In the troposphere (the layer extending up 7-10 miles above the earth's surface), ozone is a chemical oxidant and a major component of photochemical smog. Ozone can seriously affect the human respiratory system and is one of the most prevalent and widespread pollutants. Ozone in the troposphere is produced through complex chemical reactions between nitrogen oxides, which are among the primary pollutants emitted by combustion sources, hydrocarbons, which are released into the atmosphere by the combustion, handling and processing of petroleum products, and sunlight.

P

PC (Personal Computer)

The most common type of computer found in offices, classroom, or home; designed to fit on a desk and be used by one person at a time, also called a microcomputer.

Personal protective equipment

Equipment, accessories or garments used by a workman to avoid physical risk and potential infections to his body. Protective clothing keeps industrial worker clean and safe.

Pollutant

Generally, any substance introduced into the environment that has the potential to adversely affect the water, soil or air.

Pollution

Generally, the presence of matter or energy whose nature, location or quantity produces undesired environmental effects.

Q

Quality functional deployment

A way to assure the product design quality while the product is still in the design stage. It is an overall concept that provides a means of translating customer requirements into the appropriate technical requirements for each stage of product development and production. It encompasses marketing strategies, planning, product design and engineering, prototype evaluation, production process development, production, and sales.

R

Real-time

Processing of the information as it is received and provides immediate response to the input.

Re-engineering

A process of taking a broader looks, as how to re-do a system.

Renewable

Capable of being renewed or capable of being replaced by natural ecological cycles or with better management practices.

RMG

Ready Made Garment Industry.

Robotic device

An automated mechanical device or computers that performs or outputs according to previously set programme.

S

Software package

A collection of electronic instructions that direct the central processing unit of computer to carry out a specific task; created by programmers in a programming language; usually resides in computer storage.

SSI

Small scale industries.

State-of-the-art

The level of development (as of a device, procedure, process, technique, or science) reached at any particular time usually as a result of modern methods.

Sustainable development

Development that is based on factors which has in-built strength for continued maintainability. Also development that meets present needs without compromising the ability of future generations to meet their own needs.

Systems analyst

A person who creates specifications, calculates feasibility and costs, and implements a computer system. The systems analyst looks at the entire scope of a company's information-processing activities and tries to device more effective methods.

T

Total Quality Management (TQM)

This management technique refers to constant attainment of customer satisfaction through an integrated system of tools, techniques, and training. This involves continuous improvement of organisational processes, resulting in high quality products, and services. Total quality management is the way in which the organisation's culture is defined.

U

User-friendly system

An operation, programme or a computer system designed so that individual who lacks experiences or training can use the system without becoming confused or frustrated. In short a system that is easy to work with.

V

Value chain

Sequential manufacturing operations or services that adds worth to each successive step.

W

Watered capital

If the realisable value of the assets is not equal to their book value, it is said that the capital of the concern is watered. In other words, when the assets do not represent a part of its capital, the capital is watered. The company generally faces the problem of watered capital in the initial stage of its incorporation. If the capital of a company is watered it is not desirable to continue the situation for long. Management should take firm steps to correct the difference between the realisable value and the book value of the assets, and plough back a substantial part of its profits for some years.

World Wide Web (WWW)

An Internet service developed to incorporate online hypertext documents.

WTO

World Trade Organization, the internationals body dealing with the rules of trade between nations.

Bibliography

1. Automation in the Textile Industry: From Fibres to Apparel, *Berkstresser, G.A., Buchnan, D.R., and Grady, P,* 1995, The Textile Institute.

2. Beyond Quality: An Agenda for Improving Manufacturing Capabilities in Developing Countries, *Steven Wilson, Robert Balance, János Pogány,* 1995, Unido Publication, Co-publisher: Edward Elgar.

3. Case Studies in Pollution Control Measures in the Textile Dyeing and Finishing Industries, *M.H. Atkins and J.F. Lowe*, 1979, Pergamon Press.

4. Computer Systems Today (First Edition), *Suresh K. Basandra*, 1999, Wheeler Publishing.

5. Computers in the Fashion Industry, Partric Taylor, 1990, Heinemann Professional Publishing Ltd, Oxford.

6. Dye Plants and Dyeing, *Cannon, J. and M.*, 1994, Herbert Press.

7. Energy and Environment Series (1993-96), Unido Publication.

8. Engineering a New Architecture, *Robbin, T.*, 1996, Yale UP.

9. Environmental Chemistry of Dyes and Pigments, *Reife, A. and Freeman, H.S. (editors)*, 1996, Wiley.

10. Express Textiles, A Weekly Update on Textile Industry, various issues, Business Publication Division, Indian Express Group, Mumbai.

11. Fiber Science, *Steven B. Warner*, 1995, Prentice Hall.

12. Finishers and the Environment - Solutions, *Conference Papers*, 1993, The Textile Institute.

13. Five Thousands Years of Textiles, *Harris, J.*, 1993, British Museum.

14. Handbook of Fiber Science and Technology (Vol 14), *Menachem Lewin (Editor), Jack Preston (Editor), Herman F. Mark (Editor),* 1996, Marcel Dekker.

15. High-Tech Fibrous Materials: Composites, Biomedical Materials, Protective Clothing, and Geotextiles (Acs Symposium Series, No. 457),

Tyrone L. Vigo, Albin F. Turbak (Editor), 1991, Amer Chemical Society.

16. Industrial Application of Textiles (Textile Progress Vol. 6 No. 2), *Floyd, K.L. and Taylor, H.M.*, 1974, The Textile Institute.

17. Internet Resources; various web sites of machine manufaturers, textile organisations and research institutions; on-line Britannica Encyclopaedia, Compton's Encyclopaedia.

18. Introduction to Clothing manufacture, *Gerry Cooklin*, 1998, Blackwell Science Ltd, Oxford.

19. Introduction to Computers (Second Edition), *Peter Norton*, 1998, Tata McGraw-Hill Publishing Company Limited.

20. Managing Technological Change, *World Conference Papers*, 1980, The Textile Institute.

21. Manufactured Fibre Fact Book, *Fiber Economics Bureau, Inc.*, 1998, FEB Publications, Washington.

22. Natural Fibres yearbook, *Proceeding of Workshop*, 1997, Institute of Natural Fibres.

23. New Techniques in Wet Processing of Textiles, *Report of an Expert Group Meeting*, 1976, United Nations Publication.

24. On-Line Quality Control in Spinning and Weaving (Textile Progress Vol. 17 No. 1/2), *Barella, A.*, 1988, The Textile Institute.

25. Plant and Power Engineering, 1970, United Nations Publication.

26. Plant Fibre Processing: A Handbook (SSTS), *Jarman, C.*, 1998, Intermediate Technology Due.

27. Pollution Control in the Textile Industry, *Pollution Technology Review No.2*, 1973, Noyes Data Corporation, New Jersey.

28. Quick Response In Apparel Manufacturing, *Hunter, N.A.*, 1990, The Textile Institute.

29. Spinning, 1976, United Nations Publication

30. Technology Upgradation Fund Scheme for Textile and Jute Industries, 1999, Office of Textile Commissioner, Mumbai.

31. Textile Industry, Handy Manual, *Output of a Seminar on Energy Conservation in Textile Industry*, 1992, UNIDO.

32. The Book of Silk, *Scott, P.*, 1993, Thames and Hudson.

33. The International Wool Trade, *Roche, J.*, 1996, Woodhead.

34. The Production and Properties of Wool and Other Animal Fibres (Textile Progress Vol. 7 No. 3), *Ryder, M.L.*, 1975, The Textile Institute.

35. The Textile Industry and the Environment, *Technical Report No.16*,

1993, United Nations Environmental Programme.

36. Total Quality Management and Computer Integrated Manufacturing of Textiles, *Sigmon, D.M, Grady, P.L., and Winchester, S.C.*, 1998, The Textile Institute.

37. Weaving and Associated Processes, 1970, United Nations Publication

38. Winning Through Information Technology, *Conference Papers*, 1994, The Textile Institute.